DARK PSYCHOLOGY SECRETS AND MANIPULATION

*Defend Yourself from Malicious People, Detect
Deception, Brainwashing and Manipulation.
Learn Covert Manipulation Techniques,
Art of Persuasion, Self-Hypnosis,
And Mind Control for A Successful Life.*

Disclaimer Notice:

Please note the information contained within this document is for educational and entertainment purposes only. All effort has been executed to present accurate, up to date, and reliable, complete information. No warranties of any kind are declared or implied. Readers acknowledge that the author is not engaging in the rendering of legal, financial, medical or professional advice. The content within this book has been derived from various sources. Please consult a licensed professional before attempting any techniques outlined in this book.

By reading this document, the reader agrees that under no circumstances is the author responsible for any losses, direct or indirect, which are incurred as a result of the use of information contained within this document, including, but not limited to, errors, omissions, or inaccuracies.

Table of Contents

INTRODUCTION

Congratulations on buying Dark Psychology: The Secrets of Strong People the Full Guide with NLP, Manipulation, and Persuasion Methods exposing the art of reading people and getting control of their minds, and thank you for doing so.

Have you ever wondered how the individuals at the top could be where they are? Well, wonder no longer because, inside these pages, we tell you the dark psychology secrets that all successful people use to ascend to the top of the ladder. Dark psychology is the taboo branch of psychology that utilizes its studies to unravel, read, and mold the human mind to our advantage.

Mind reading and mind control are not imaginary activities, but if you use the methods taught in Dark Psychology, they are achievable. Read on to learn the forbidden wisdom required for someone in today's cutthroat world who wants to not only survive but succeed.

This book has everything you need to get a handle on dark psychology and all its applications, including mind-reading, mind control, manipulation of actions, and more. Without being caught, you'll also learn how to trick others, protect yourself against other manipulators, and use these tactics in real environments like at work.

Learning the dark side of psychology has never been simpler. These chapters are detailed yet succinct, as they are filled with the experience you need to be the best at everything you do. If you work in an office, with the community, or in the arts, it doesn't matter. In dark psychology, both of us have stuff we can experience that will make our lives a whole lot easier.

From here, all it takes is to read on, and you will have every tool required to bend the will of another to your material. There are plenty of books on the market on this topic; thanks again for selecting this one! Every effort has been made to ensure that as much valuable knowledge as possible is plentiful. Enjoy! Enjoy!

CHAPTER ONE:

WHAT IS DARK PSYCHOLOGY?

Owing to social ties, genes, or pure luck, it can be tempting to believe that specific individuals do better in life than others. But the fact is they only know how the human mind can be exploited. If they learned it from a friend, read it in a novel, or knew how to instinctively pick up on it, dark psychology was the secret to all the triumphs of their lives.

There is nothing but an awareness of dark psychology that ultimately distinguishes you from them. The depths of psychology they do not want you to know are explored in this chapter. The key to transforming your future for good is to discover these mysteries of psychology. It's not something that many people like to accept, but in fact, it's not typically because of chance, genes, generational wealth, or any of these variables that make certain people more successful. Otherwise, why are there individuals as strong as those born into it who actually had to earn it?

This theory does not tell us why certain people are more successful than others at the end of the day. But there's one thing we can all do to better our lives, and it's to learn how to communicate in a different way with people. Learning how to interact effectively with individuals will change everything for you.

Dark psychology isn't just going to show you how to interact casually with people the way everyone does. We are talking about the types of communication that alter the power balance: the types of communication that allow people to achieve their goals. If you are an ambitious person, the only road to the success you are looking for is dark psychology. In a way that seems "fair" to us, almost all of us want to get ahead, but this is a troublesome way of thinking about it.

That is because, to our benefit, there is nothing unjust about using unique communication methods. All that dark psychology really does for us is to teach us how to communicate with people in the most efficient way possible in the form of coercion, persuasion, and mind control. It can turn anything around in spite of its simplicity. You probably also think of manipulation as an instrument used by evil people to accomplish their objectives.

You may even have reservations about it, believing you're not supposed to use coercion yourself. But what its prestige has won for itself is not deception at all. Manipulation is a neutral word: it implies that we have modified the actions of others. You might think that reading the mind and manipulating the mind are both terrible things, but they are not. Much like manipulation, both of them are neutral. Mind reading is breaking someone's brain's code and finding out what they think secretly. Mind control gets into their brain and does more than reading it. What's there is shifting.

It would make sense, from an intuitive perspective, to think that these things are ethically dubious. But once you understand how all three of these techniques are actually used under our noses on a constant basis, we recognize that there is nothing wrong with using the laws of psychology to assist us, particularly when someone else can get to us first.

Soon, without even realizing it, we will get into the ways in which all three of these activities find their way into our everyday lives. But you can understand, for the time being, why we think they're ethically neutral and not either good or bad.

Mind reading, mind control, and deception are not things that are evil or unethical, but no matter what we plan to do, they will always happen. From time to time, we already do all of this stuff ourselves, and we already have them used on us in particular. The only difference is that you will know how to use them in an intentional, insightful way when you learn how to use them in this book. You're not going to need to be in the dark about how other people use it on you. When anyone is taking advantage of you, you will be able to say.

Meanwhile, to step up in life, you would be able to use the strategies for yourself. To do so, there is no justification. You have to use it to hurt someone else. How you use the abilities that you gain in these chapters is solely your decision. We have said that our questions about coercion and mind control in dark psychology can teach us about communication. A lot of dark psychology and manipulation beginners think that this means we're just going to learn about social psychology's dark side and no other area.

This is far from reality, however. There are dark aspects in every branch of psychology, and they all have thoughts in them that we can use in mind-reading and manipulation to our advantage. It's your decision whether you keep reading or not if you really don't feel able to move on, knowing that we're getting into dark territory. However, if you put this book down, all the dark truths of psychology that will make you an adept manipulator and mind reader right off the bat will be missed.

We told you what dark psychology is in theory, but now in the history of psychology, you can read about some examples of it. There were studies that were controversial or produced controversial results, but today we can use and apply these findings to our lives. The fact that they tread into dark territories doesn't mean that we shouldn't use them. The truths that no one wants to remember are perhaps the most important ones of all.

The ethical rules on psychiatric research were much laxer no more than fifty to sixty years ago. These days, before you can conduct an official experiment, your work needs to jump through a lot of bureaucratic hoops to be accepted by the American Psychological Association. The APA is really strict about upholding a code of ethical principles, and if it doesn't meet their moral standards, your work won't even be written.

But no such standards existed around the 1970s or before. It's because psychology was a new social science that started to be taken seriously just then. There wasn't enough precedent for a code of rules or an organization like the APA to be created. As a result, many of the studies carried out at this time will be deemed to violate far too many ethical rules for the expectations of today. Many of them are not going to be released today.

Even since they have plenty to teach us about psychology, these studies are still being studied. But the term dark psychology is given to it because of the controversial subject matter and the possible harmful use of this field of psychology. It's time to dig into the real case studies and tests in dark psychology, with the introduction out of the way.

The first experiment of our kind dates back to 1939. A group of orphans from a foster home followed, all of whom had impediments to speech.

A house of orphans was sorted into two distinct groups by the psychologist: one of the orphan groups went to live in a nurturing community.

In science research, if you don't already know the terms, when you give different conditions to two groups, there are different words for each group. The control group is called the group that goes through normal conditions. We use the control group to compare it against the other group and see whether there was some measurable difference between the groups as a result of their setting.

The other group, the experimental group, went to live in deliberately hostile settings in this situation. They were raised with foster families who were abusive physically and emotionally. If this sounds terrible to you, note that it was only because it was 1939 that this was allowed to happen. The APA did not even exist yet, so there was no one to warn the scientists that this experiment was not supposed to be performed.

It shows us a lot, considering how bad this therapy was, and that sums up dark psychology quite a bit. You see, when the psychologists looked at the differences between the control group that lived in a positive atmosphere and the pessimistic study group, the children of the two groups noticed something completely different.

At the beginning of the analysis, both groups of orphans had a large number of kids who had speech impediments. The orphans with restrictions to speech that belonged to the control group either did not improve their speech or improved marginally. However, in the negative environment, the orphans in the experimental community did not improve; they got worse overall.

In the experimental group, the average verbal scores for the orphans were substantially lower than the mean scores for the orphans in the control group.

This shows us our first dark psychology lesson. There should be no underestimation of the influence of our social climate. With children, of course, this is especially true. But the impact on adults of the social setting is also profound. This causes us to be sad when we feel like we don't belong, not to be our best. It makes us feel like we don't have to offer something, and we don't even see the point of doing anything. These feelings are the reason why the orphans in the experimental community did not strengthen their speech. It wasn't because the children in the supportive settings had better teachers: what made this possible was the various emotional atmospheres.

As you try to learn how to mold someone's mind to your advantage, note this finding in dark psychology. Whenever you have the chance to deception the social climate of the topic in a way that will help you, take it. All this suggests that individuals are extremely driven to alter their social circumstances. They will take it if they see a chance to climb up the social ladder. For everyone, it works this way. Before you can do this, you still have more theory and skills to master, but a large portion of the skeleton of dark psychology and manipulation is this: if you make anyone believe that it will boost their social status to perform a certain action or follow a particular ideology, they will do it. To us, our social status is just that important.

Our social lives are, as human beings, among the most important things for us. In fact, alongside water, food, shelter, our need to belong, and socializing is considered one of our needs. One of the pieces of evidence you can take advantage of by researching dark psychology is understanding how vulnerable people are to feeling depressed and set aside. You are able to move on to the following foundational lesson of dark psychology with that in mind.

This discovery in dark psychology caught the imagination of so many people that, despite dark psychology being so taboo, you've probably heard of it. Often when the details are too captivating to look away from, even prohibited information is talked around. The bystander effect is called this observation.

Another case includes this field of dark psychology that shows us the importance of social forces. Essentially, it is the well-supported belief that people are going to watch something bad happen to others and not do something; they prefer not to do something because they know that there are a lot of other people around them. Since there are so many people around them, these bystanders believe that there is no reason for them to do anything; someone else can call the police or rescue the victim.

We know that the bystander effect is basically a field of dark psychology that gets its origins from a part of normal psychology: in particular, it arises because of a process called social responsibility diffusion. Even if you have not seen anything tragic happening around a large group of people, sometime in your life, you have certainly seen the diffusion of social responsibility before. When they are part of a team or band, most individuals see this psychological effect in action.

For instance, when you are part of a team, you might see the ball coming your way. But you see that three of your teammates are with you; thinking one of them is coming to get the ball, you're going to back off and get ready for the next step of the game. The four of you, however, have the same feeling, and no one claims the ball. The other squad ends up with it.

DARK PSYCHOLOGY SECRETS AND MANIPULATION

You get a general idea: it helps us feel less guilty for doing it ourselves when we believe other people are going to do something. Another large part of it is where dark psychology weaves its way into the propagation of social responsibility as well: people would find every reason for doing less work. If we don't need to do something, we would still prefer to do less work. The belief that someone else can take care of an obligation gives us an excuse not to do it ourselves.

With that, you have two big ideas in your mind in Dark Psychology. These are far from the only dark psychology examples you're going to hear about, so keep reading for more. From here on out, we will apply what we know to the manipulation and regulation of the minds of people in this field of psychology.

Solipsism and Human Behavior

Now that you are familiar with the dark psychology world, it is time for you to dive into its actual application. You picked up this book, after all, so you could learn how to read and influence minds, exploit the actions of other people, efficiently trick people, and step up in your career. We will explain the path to do all these things; all it takes is to take the main concepts we learn and apply them to real-life situations.

In Dark Psychology, the first important thing for us to understand is about normal human narcissism. From a broad research base, we know that humans are self-centered and narcissistic. Don't take this to mean that we are greedy in a manner that hurts others in any conceivable case. In this grim of a way, it does not have to be taken. However, it is real that all of us think of our own needs instinctively before anyone else's. Getting over this obstacle of narcissism takes a lot of preparation and schooling.

You can use this human vulnerability to your advantage, as a learner of dark psychology and as a manipulator. You know that narcissistic people are so feeding your egos. Many people are scared to look like they are brown-nosed, but we know that this result from dark psychology generally won't come across this way because of it.

You see, it is not self-centeredness or narcissism that is the scientific term for this human trait. It's about solipsism. Solipsism is a concept that goes deeper than just thinking about yourself highly and not thinking about other people much. Solipsism is the quality that we all have to some degree, which suggests that we do not really grasp the point of view of anyone else.

The bulk of the world's individuals are not real solipsists. Most of us, to some extent, understand the fact that there are other individuals and that they have their own experiences. There is a distinction, however, between recognizing this reality and understanding it profoundly. Many of the people you meet in the world are not completely capable of understanding the dignity of others. That's too much to fathom for them, so they remain in their own little personal world, where it all makes sense. It is easier to get into their minds and change what you see in them with this solipsistic characteristic. It makes them vulnerable to reading, mind control, and manipulation of minds.

It is difficult to tell to decide how many real solipsists are out there. We are not talking about the typical person when we say "true solipsist," who gets the impression that other people are almost like them but don't really get it. We are talking about individuals who, for whatever reason, are never aware of someone else's experience. They may not have been raised to read a lot of stories as a child, which is supposed to improve your empathy. Maybe certain individuals are simply programmed in such a way that prevents them from recognizing the viewpoint of other individuals. There are certain individuals out there who are quick to use dark psychology either way because they are so involved in their own little worlds that they are oblivious to deception.

This is good news, but there is something to bear in mind that is important. The bulk of individuals who are worth exploiting are not solipsists. It makes sense because, by definition, if you are a solipsist, you are greedy and unable to comprehend the point of view of anyone else. An attitude like that doesn't help you get closer and build trust with people.

However, it doesn't mean you can't use solipsism with your average person to your benefit. Far from it, in fact. Even if the majority of people out there aren't real solipsists, we are all human beings, and we have a solipsistic hand. This oblivious and self-centered component of your subject's psyche clearly has to be taken out and used to your advantage.

In a number of forms, Solipsism shows itself. One way to think about it is this: we kind of have to be greedy at the end of the day. We can't spend all our time taking into account the views of others. We would not be able to survive if we did that. There is a cut-off point where we have to decide for ourselves what is best to do.

This leads to several mental shortcuts and cognitive prejudices, which are concepts that we're going to get to later on. Our minds, essentially, don't like confusion. Our minds need to feel that they truly understand the universe, or else they would not be able to turn it off. For a significant number of things, the human brain is responsible, so it does not waste a whole lot of time thinking deeply and imagining experiences outside of itself.

It must then rationalize for itself that there is nothing that it does not comprehend. All makes sense in the little mental universe that it creates; it feels safe. You have to be cautious when venturing deeper into someone's mind as a student of dark psychology. Since our minds have the need to assume that they understand everything, people challenging their assumptions don't take it well. They're not going to invite you into their headspace if you swoop into challenging all your subject believes. This is not to suggest that there is nothing you can ever doubt. It's just that you need to be mindful of time and place. There will be no problems with ruffling people's feathers too much if you follow the instructions we provide you with. You won't have any problems as long as you do things in the correct order and when the subject is ready.

You need to first make them feel like you're not going to challenge their views of the universe until you challenge any solipsist, whether they're genuine solipsists or just an average individual with a normal amount of solipsism. It may sound like it's not going to help you break into their heads, but it's about doing the right things in the right order again. They won't ever let you into their headspace if you don't get them to trust you first. The first step is always the establishment of confidence. You must affirm the ideas of this individual's world to build trust between the two of you. If you think their thoughts are correct or skewed, it doesn't matter. Initially, you have to make them see you as someone who blends into their little mental world before you do anything else. Only with dark psychology can you do something else from here.

The second step comes after this, and you have to fit your world concepts into their current worldview. You'll be intimately informed about how they perceive the world after you have formed a bond with them, and they trust you, so you know what will fit and what will not fit.

How to do this is not always clear. Often no matter how imaginative you want to be, it seems like someone's ideas about stuff just won't mesh with yours. It takes time for two objects to fit together that at first seem not to want to fit. This is much better with a genuine solipsist than with someone else. This is because you will not have to do anything else as long as they see your thoughts and theirs as able to co-exist. Their brain's version of truth thinks that without being questioned, it will proceed, which is what a solipsist needs.

A typical person with partial solipsism is a little trickier. Along with your feelings, they have their brain's vision of the universe; but in addition to these, they have some idea of other views that exist in the world. They're not entirely like the real solipsist because they're going to equate the views with other ideas they've encountered in the world as well.

By getting really close to them, you can always get them to believe what you are asking them. This is why modifying the thoughts and actions of someone who is not a complete solipsist takes much longer. With them, it's not as easy as fitting a puzzle piece into their puzzle of mind that fits: they have some idea of the outside world and all the ideas besides yours that exist.

But with the concepts of dark psychology explained in this book, if you want to exploit their actions or mind control them to have new beliefs, you can still succeed in tinkering with their minds. It all comes down to blurring their perceived conceptual boundaries between you and themselves. The next segment shows you exactly how to do this. You are able to use this experience to discover the mysteries of dark psychology and the methods that will help you progress in your career and social life, with the concepts and history of dark psychology under your belt.

CHAPTER TWO:

SECRETS AND STRATEGIES OF DARK PSYCHOLOGY

The methods and secrets used by the power of the World to conquer cultures and nations are included in these pages. Although the previous chapter provided you with a theoretical deception work for dark psychology, these concepts are put into practice in this Chapter.

It's as straightforward to break into someone's mind as using the power of words, but you do need to know the correct words to use. That is why it is primarily a matter of practicing your vocabulary to learn how to use dark psychology in real life, so it can open up the mind of someone else. There are countless methods to learn, but in fact, you only need a few to break into the mind of someone. Let's start off. Good people follow the first of three important steps for successful persuasion, mind control, and mind-reading.

You need to know you are in control of yourself before you do something. You need to know that whatever the subject does would not negatively impact you. You might be shocked at how difficult it is to do this. There is a fair risk that you will crash into a wall until you finally get ready for your first attempt at breaking into someone's mind. This wall is the way you are emotionally, verbally, behaviorally, and more influenced by the subject. You won't be able to break into their heads if the subject affects you. If this happens, they are the ones getting into your mind. Scientists who research the brain or neuroscientists now understand the explanation for this. In our minds, this comes down to a particular kind of neuron called mirror neurons. Mirror neurons were discovered in an accident when neuroscientists were examining chimps. The way they function is actually effortless, considering how many implications mirror neurons have.

The neuroscientists scanned two individual chimps' brains. When this unique neuron (the mirror neuron) began to fire into their brain, the first chimp was carrying a banana. How the other chimp blends into the photo are an interesting aspect. The other chimpanzee itself did not hold a banana: they merely watched the other chimpanzee hold the banana, but despite this, the very same special neuron shot.

This led to the accidental discovery of mirror neurons by neuroscientists. Mirror neurons are now understood as the neurons that allow our brains to imagine actions, whether they are real actions that we are doing or only actions that we imagine. What makes mirror neurons so amazing is that we don't really have to do something to get the same response from our mirror neurons. They'll shoot either way.

You may extend this to a multitude of things: our mirror neurons go off as if we are reading chips when we read a novel, and the character eats chips. The way our brains understand the meanings of things is through mirror neurons. Scientists are postulating that we have evolved to mirror neurons in order to plan for the future. We may not be doing an action right now, but when we watch an action, our minds are planning to actually do it in the future. The function of mirror neurons is this. Now you have already found out how this already relates to mind control and coercion because it can still begin to affect you when you see the subject being emotional. It feels like a social force that makes us want to get along with them emotionally.

While social factors undoubtedly play into it because of neuroscience, we now know that the research that contributes to this happens in the brain.

Not only do we feel socially forced to communicate feelings in reaction to people in our lives, but our mirror neurons are firing in response to the actions of the person. Even if they are the ones doing the behavior, our mirror neurons are firing just as theirs are, and you are just experiencing it.

That's what makes it so difficult to control ourselves in the manner that is required to become competent in mind reading, mind control, and manipulation. There is a neuroscientific and biological process that leads us to be affected by them.

But we don't want to accept being influenced by our subject, as we said. We are expected to manipulate them, and that's when it comes to state power. State management is the first skill you have to master if you want to succeed in these dark psychology applications. Essentially, at any moment, it is your right to convey whatever feelings you need to feel. It is your ability not to be impacted by the mirror neurons of strangers but to be able to select what feelings you express at any moment instead.

For you to learn, it is the first ability because it prevents you from being the focus. You see, they expect us to be affected by them when we communicate with individuals, if not all the time. By listening to the advice of other dark psychology books, don't go about learning state power the wrong way. By giving them the false impression of state power, they confuse readers.

State regulation, for one thing, does not mean you stop feeling emotions. State regulation means being able to manage your thoughts, and this is far from the same thing.

And when we say that to avoid being affected by the issue, you should use state regulation, that doesn't mean that you should never react in a way that would be typical of normal social interaction. In reality, much of the time, you can find that in the same exchange, you can always express feelings as the average person would.

The distinction that state control makes is that it allows you the right to choose when and how you emotionally respond. You should react in the socially anticipated way most of the time, and sometimes you shouldn't. It all depends on how you can balance walking the line between matching the brain of the subject's wavelengths and manipulating your objectives. We'll be talking more about this later, but back to state power for now.

As we said, state control, regardless of the emotional stimulation surrounding them, is often wrongly thought of as one's ability to display no emotion. But since this is the most valuable emotion to communicate, it is really one's ability to express any feeling at any time. You can't hope to do this by doing the way you usually would all the time when you want the subject to do something or change their beliefs. Sometimes, depending on what advantages the attempt at coercion or mind control benefits, you may have to adjust your own emotions. The toughest part of state control is that you could do so at any moment on purpose. To learn some capacity to control your thoughts, you don't have to research dark psychology. In fact, we have no choice but to get better and better at this ability as we grow up and become adults to learn to become part of society.

It can help you see that it is possible to fully replace your natural emotions with a new one by understanding that you have already mastered how to temper your emotions. You know now why it matters to state power, so how do you achieve it? Something called anchoring is the solution.

Anchoring has a long-range of uses; it is also a tool you can use in mind control and manipulation. However, in the sense of state power, it is the tactic you use at any point during your relationship with the subject to take command of your emotional speech.

By tapping into your imagination, the process of anchoring helps you to do this. As adults, we sometimes make the mistake of thinking about creativity in childhood as something to be left behind. When we read a book or watch a TV series, the more open-minded amongst us may see it as something reserved for. But the fact is, creativity goes far beyond our lives in these places. Imagination is how the solipsist in us would assume that, amid all the contradictory evidence around us, we understand the universe most of the time, which may make us doubt that.

Don't underestimate the force, even as an adult, of imagination. Anchoring depends strongly on creativity. The fact that Aristotle suggested using creativity as a way to remain on track to accomplish our goals and do the things we claim we want to do is one thing that might redeem the definition of imagination for you. And what he proposed was anchoring, in essence.

Aristotle said that in your mind, the day before you do a job, imagine doing the task. In order to achieve the mission, don't only imagine completing the task in general, but instead, imagine all the little tasks you would have to do. Aristotle said that if we were to do this before bed every night, we would really do the stuff we imagined we were doing the next day. This is because we have already seen it in our brains, so it stops us from being intimidated the way we would generally be. It is not so different when we use anchoring to accomplish state power. The biggest difference is simply because it can be very difficult to manipulate a person, so we have to put a lot of stuff into the anchoring to be prepared for a variety of circumstances.

To get started, pick one feeling that you want to be prepared to convey at will with your face. First, think about a time when you really felt this sensation, and do your hardest to remember how that feeling actually felt. Keep doing this with all the critical feelings until, at any moment, you can call an emotion you want to feel and show it on your face.

The last move is exactly the same as what was said by Aristotle. You now have all the feelings at your hands, so think about all the different directions your attempt could go as the subject could be exploited. For all of these opportunities, react with the required emotion. You can't be prepared for every single little thing, of course.

It will build your confidence, though, and you're not going to be so discouraged that you're not going to try, and even if things come up that you didn't expect, you were prepared for other things that happened, so you're not going to be overwhelmed. You will have more of a cognitive load to be ready for it, and you will respond accordingly.

Anchoring is not the only way of achieving control of the state. You should try other helpful approaches, so you can see which one suits you best. The simplest form of all is deep breathing. We feel more comfortable because we have more oxygen in our bodies, and our brains also function better.

Sadly, it's normal for individuals to assume that deep breathing is only breathing more slowly, but that's not what it is. You feel the air moving deeper into your body as you breathe deeply.

If you can sense the air going as far in as it can go, don't let yourself believe that you are deep breathing, hence the term deep breathing. This state control approach does not assist you in conveying particular emotions such as anchoring, but often the most complex part does not respond to the emotions expressed by the subject, and this is most useful for that.

When you do this, the other important thing to remember is not to breathe so loudly that you look suspicious. You don't want your subject to ring any warning bells because if they notice you're breathing loudly, they'll still be suspicious, though they probably won't suspect you're trying to influence or manipulate your mind.

No matter what stimuli you are given, the last technique for learning state control will help you remain calm. There is more than one way to learn how to suppress your emotions while you are interacting with others, but this one is the easiest to practice at any time, any place.

The definition of an actor "breaking character" during a scene is probably familiar to you. This suggests that the actor felt that another actor's line or gesture was so amusing that they came out of the scene and were about to laugh. What you are trying to learn is basically very close to not "breaking character" when you learn state power.

The character you play is the individual who does all the right things for you to get the data you need from the subject, or to influence or exploit them, regardless of your objective. With this mentality, either go through online videos or look at comedy options on any streaming platforms that you may have. Make sure you find something most of the time that will really make you laugh. By watching these without laughing, you can exercise state regulation or not "breaking character." For learning state regulation, this is a very great exercise. No matter how amusing the scene or actor is, the final aim should be to look like a brick wall.

Suppressing a joke from your laughter is not precisely the same thing as not showing feelings no matter what the subject offers you, but they are practically the same. You have to accept the same sensory data that most days will make you respond in a certain way, and you have to choose not to react to it. Anchoring will also help you get stronger with deep breathing and this exercise.

The first of three stages of effective mind control and manipulation is state control. It is also the most important move, because as we have said: if at any given time you cannot choose how you display your feelings, you are the one who is affected. You can't claim to have any control over them as long as you give up this power to the subject.

As we move along in the book, we will get into steps 2 and 3, but as you read on, note this important fact: steps 2 and 3 are where the mind control and conditioning strategies come in. With these methods alone, though, you won't be able to pull off reasonable attempts. They are not like recipes for cookbooks, where you simply follow the instructions in the correct order and get the desired outcome. Before you can succeed with them, you will need to have basic skills like state control. Speaking of which, before moving to steps 2 and 3, there is one more important skill that you must master before using the techniques we will soon teach you.

Perceptual sharpness is called this ability. The other half of the first level of mind control and manipulation is perceptual sharpness. It is a concept that is not unique to the field of dark psychology. In virtually any skill you can think of, whether you are thinking about cooking, repairing stuff, healthcare, academia, and much more, strong perceptual sharpness is useful. This is because it means that all perceptual sharpness is how powerful the senses are. The more you see, hear, smell, taste, and feel, the better you have perceptual acuity.

First of all, with all of your simple senses, you can determine your abilities. Have you ever been advised that you have an outstanding sense of smell? Are you capable of finding objects quickly by touching them? Do you instantly know when a celebrity you know is a TV voice actor? Does your eye automatically catch tiny details wherein the first place, most people will never even recognize them?

Perceptual sharpness can be a good skill to have no matter what discipline you study, but it is particularly important in dark psychology. You have to be able to pick up a lot of data quickly while you are in conversation with the subject. You see more details about your topic you can get the better. The quicker you can get the results, the better.

Your senses are essentially the most effective resources at your disposal. They are your way into the world beyond the world in which you and your subject live. You may be used to going through life without worrying too much about the contents of your surroundings, but that must end today. A big reason not everyone can learn dark psychology, after all, is that they miss all the tiny details. You can't help but note the little details when you have good perceptual sharpness. That's why perceptual sharpness is just as vital as regulation of the state. You definitely need control of the state so you don't become the one who is mind-controlled. But what will give you the advantage is your perceptual sharpness. Early on, it will make you privy to data that the subject never believes you know in the first place. The more you know that you know without thinking about the issue, the better.

And the strength of our perceptive sharpness comes at the end of the day from the wealth of experience that it can provide us. Not just any details: we are talking explicitly about information relating to the subject. In engaging with the subject, the most important thing you can do at any stage is to collect more information about them. The more of them you know, the better. However, at the same time, you don't want them to know that you're constantly and actively searching for information about them as a person. Fortunately, perceptual sharpness makes it possible, so we don't have to sneak around for that data. People send us information without really thinking about it all the time, and with perceptual information, we will naturally absorb the data.

In combination with another talent that is something of a buzzword lately, perceptual sharpness works with active listening. Nowadays, they say active listening is uncommon, but the fact is, it's always been rare. Because of our understanding of dark psychology, we know to the degree that individuals are all solipsists. We care a lot for ourselves, and for the most part, we care just for the world beyond ourselves in terms of how it applies to us.

We use this to our benefit as learners of dark psychology and manipulators. All we have to do in a casual conversation is get people to chat. Ask questions that give you the data you need. Just make sure that you do it in a way that seems casual and unassuming.

This is how you get away with gathering as much information as you can about the subject. Like we said, as a manipulator, this is the biggest way you can support yourself: get more information about the topic.

A vital aspect of active listening, however, is auditory sharpness. Over the decades, several writers have told us that instead of only engaging in the dialog to hear ourselves talking, we need to do a better job of listening. But how can we be effective with active listening? Instead of tuning out the way people prefer to do, how do we retrieve and recall the details the subject gives us?

Sharpness in vision. This is the key to effective listening actively. Think about how you should adapt these methods to the sense of active listening when we delve through the ways in which you can maximize your perceptual sharpness since this is where your objectives would be most beneficial. First, answer the first hurdle of achieving strong sensitivity of perception. This barrier does not make it a target in the first place. That means you can, as a priority, go through all your experiences with your senses. This involves interactions with individuals other than the subject, as it is the only way you can get into the habit of doing it.

It requires consciously asking yourself the habits you find in the subject to resolve this first hurdle. How do they make use of body language? Just get detailed. How far are their feet apart? Have they got a calm posture? Are they breathing slowly or rapidly? But this is just the first impediment. The next one is to consciously stop doing this. Without talking to yourself, you want the senses to do this by themselves.

Without you standing in their way, the senses actually do a better job. We instruct you to consciously tell them what to do first so that, first of all, you become capable of listening to your senses. Yet, you want to stop getting in their way until you are used to listening to your feelings. Stop overthinking the data you get from your senses, and simply take in all the data you get. In a novel, this may sound weird, all about something as profound as dark psychology, mind control, and coercion, but you have to turn your brain off to get to the highest degree of perceptual sharpness. You don't want the senses to put more effort into it. You don't need to. Without you involved at all, the senses automatically do their work. Passively accept the data they supply you with and let that be the end of it. When you hit this level of perceptual sharpness, both jobs will be easier.

You will be prepared to penetrate the subject's mind and do what you please from there with state regulation and perceptual sharpness working together. To this end, you can read on to find out more about using dark psychology.

CHAPTER THREE:

THE ESSENCE OF DARK PSYCHOLOGY

Psychology has sought to uplift the human spirit in recent years with several common psychological concepts such as "Positive Psychology" or the various books published to tell the masses how to act from talking about parachutes, ten steps to something the mired of how to" titles, and much more to lead a fulfilled happy life. Any of them is nothing but misplaced pop psychology or a fad of the moment. Can existence be as simple as reading the right book and following certain universal principles, and for you and me, everything will be OK? We will discuss the "Dark" side of the human mind—that part that sees disengagement, devastation, vile actions as part of the regular human psyche that occurs from time to time in us all—that part that finds passion, joy, and enjoyment in the dysfunctional part of our life. This paper is different. How can society, with its dark side, be reconciled? To refer to those in society who contradict the social norm, I use the word crazy.

Dark Psychology is both the study of criminal & deviant behavior and a psychological structure within all human beings to decode the capacity for evil. Dark Psychology is the study of the human condition as it relates to the psychological essence of individuals driven by criminal and/or deviant drives that lack intent and general assumptions of instinctual drives and the theory of social sciences to manipulate other individuals. In order to victimize other individuals and living beings, all of mankind has this ability. However, this urge is restrained or sublimated by many, some act upon these impulses. Dark Psychology attempts to explain certain emotions, feelings, beliefs, and mechanisms of subjective processing that contribute to a predatory activity that is antithetical to human behavior's contemporary understandings. Dark Psychology presumes that 99% of the time, criminal, deviant, and violent actions are deliberate and have some logical, goal-oriented motivation. It is the remaining 1 percent of the pieces of Adlerian theory and the teleological method, Dark Psychology. Inside the human mind, Dark Psychology postulates that there is an area that causes certain individuals to perform atrocious actions without intent. In this philosophy, the Dark Singularity has been coined.

Next, let's explore how the "Dark Side" of psychological thinking and conduct can be defined. We need a metric to know what is normal and what is considered abnormal activity. Social norms are our first measure; this means what is considered a standard daily activity in every society given a collection of circumstances that confront our understanding. For example, striking another person violently in Western culture is considered a criminal act and one that is repugnant to a peaceful society. However, when the individual is granted social permits such as a soldier in the act of war, a policeman in the act of arrest of a violent suspect, a citizen protecting his family from another person's serious threat, we condone abuse. It is possible to misunderstand these double standards in many ways. The soldier who commits war crimes such as genocide, the police officer who uses abuse to threaten a witness while questioning them, or the individual who abuses the rights of another person in order to in any way advance their own status.

Is the second measure moral? How do we determine what is right and wrong as a society, who has the authority to decide these rights, do laws follow moral conviction, or do they become the defense of the weak against the strong or the rich against the poor? Most communities accept that it is against a moral code to murder another human being—it is inherently unethical to kill and should be punishable by an act of equal severity, by a culture that accepts the moral-legal stance imposed by its politicians on the masses. For most cultures, this was a moral code of conduct from Buddhism to the Muslim Koran, such as the ten commandments of the Christian faith and other such codes. In the legal language and rules are seen as the basis of every civilized nation of individuals, trust in divine reward and punishment is expressed. Having embraced these rules, why then do people easily deviate from these morals, laws, and religious rules that allow us all to live in a safe community governed by agreed behavioral standards that protect the person from threat, harm, and abuse?

The third field of conduct is that it is not set out in law or religious concepts, but in certain regular sets of conduct that English might refer to as "manners" or "polite" The conduct or way of behaving that conforms to actions recognized as that of a superior member of a society who knows how to conduct themselves in the company of others to a set of norms that are seen as the mark of an advanced civilization. Sometimes this can be seen in the etiquette of table manners or a man opening a door for a woman and allowing her to enter first, acknowledging the duty of a man to protect and defend women. Today, women's rights have cast doubt on manners towards women as discriminatory in some societies and thereby degrading the independence of a woman.

Nevertheless, manners, whether standard English or a Japanese tea ceremony, are seen as the symbol of being well-bread and in the upper echelons of society.

Having developed cultures with various ways of measuring actions, human beings still handle a wide variety of dysfunctional behavior that often affects and affects others to the degree that the perpetrators of this behavior are beyond the law, moral codes, and etiquette of the rest of society. Sometimes through the feeling of remorse, we all realize when we have transgressed those laws that we see as important to a well-ordered society. However, when faced with dealing with violence, devastation, and death against others, there are those other individuals who feel nothing as merely their right to live without those rules and the freedom to live a life that is defined by nothing more than what they want to own, possess or kill.

The Dark-side

What does the man who kicks the dog possess when he is annoyed by the culture that conceals his life? When the dog screeches and howls in pain and terror, what emotions does he release at that moment? Why is he laughing and wishing the further dog harm and loving the sight of an animal in pain? On-lookers are outraged by his actions and sympathy for the defenseless dog this man has tried to handle without remorse and cruelly. Who's the man here? Why, from time to time, he is one of us. When we grapple with life's unfairness or lack of opportunity, we all lose our sense of psychological calm and sound ideas. On the other side—wait—because this man is rich, has satisfied all his needs, but still feels great pleasure in kicking and watching the dog suffer at his hands. A sense of power in his ability to cause pain and the satisfaction of feeling superior to those inferior humans whom he sees as unable to take what they want and thus end up with

37

his staff and servants. This singular positional thought leads to a lack of sympathy or empathy towards others, as only fools who, as leaders and politicians, embrace the superiority of their kind.

The above example is to provide an insight into conduct that violates our three social norms, moral law (hurting a defenseless animal), socially acceptable behavior (the taboo on senseless behavior perceived as wrongdoing), socially acceptable behavior (while everyone might lose their temper and kick their dog, most will feel pangs of guilt and remorse). Here, however, we meet individuals who feel no shame, no regret, and see themselves as excluded from laws that they disagree with. Was fox-hunting a cruel sport mostly carried out by smart, professional, wealthy men and women in England? Yet, for nothing more than a good time, the same people demanded the right to hunt and destroy a defenseless animal when they watched their hounds rip apart and devour a fox. It took several years of lobbying to have this enacted into law, but the majority of English citizens voted on several occasions to ban this sport. Fox-hunting is now an illegal practice, but these same individuals continue to breach the law and hunt under local by-laws that have failed to comply with national legislation. These people know what they are doing is illegal, immoral, and against social norms, as defined by majority opinion. Yet, they claim to be superior members of society and therefore above the common masses' regular moral concerns. The exciting thing in England is that these individuals are members of parliament, police, judges, and those who regulate facets of English cultures, such as property owners (land given often by Royal consent in the past by robbing the rightful land of the poor).

In other words, the same people who should set an example for society are the very people who flaunt the rules and conduct that are socially acceptable.

In another case, we've got to look at a suspect. As they have come from flawed backgrounds, impoverished homes, and inadequate parental education, offenders are also seen as the rejects of society. Yet, in culture, a corporate crime such as pension fund embezzlement, securities, and shares in insider trading and theft of assets and resources by CEOs and government officials is also the greatest damage done to the public. Sometimes this so-called white-collar crime is undetected and the most difficult to bring to justice. As their offenses trigger localized distress and make the media scream for police action and civil authority action, everyday offenders are more visual to the public.

Therefore most laws that are easy to understand and understand are about visual crime. Visual crime punishment is also straightforward and dealt with in our courts and media every day. The so-called victimless crime of white-collar criminals who see no direct victim or the murderer who kills and maims those who oppose his will to steal what he wants from society and the distress they leave behind during an armed robbery: how do we distinguish between the two types of criminal?

So what does psychology have to say about deviants who do not see their behavior as an issue for themselves and feel that others do not take control of their lives as weak and therefore deserve to be victims of those who are smarter, stronger, or more powerful? The media often cries out about the passive masses that accept the status quo, and the local person who took the law into their own hands might be condemned in the same document to avenge some wrongdoing against them or their families? The first area that the reasons behind this dark behavior of others are explained by psychology is "developmental" that upbringing is on the path of this behavior, that the dog-kicker was not correctly loved or cared for. That they were subject to cruelty, sexual abuse, or lack of social education during their formative years.

That the same transgressors were victims of bullying at school and thus needed to carry out their own anger on others in society that is weaker than themselves, the question we have to ask here is why some victims, in fact, most, continue to be law-abiding citizens and it is only the few who for reasons of developmental errors, turn into monsters who kill and maim? Many scientists like to point to a genetic factor in behavior at this stage. For some time now, this old chestnut has been around. There is evidence that violent criminals often have an extra Y chromosome (men) that gives them a high amount of testosterone, leading to violent outbursts in frustrating situations where they use terror and fear as the key to getting what they need. However, as a percentage of violent criminals, this is statistically minute, even though this may be greater in the general prison population. So far, all genetic research has led to speculation about genetic factors, but with no solid evidence to support the allegations. The evidence most frequently cited is that twin studies in which twins separated at birth have a high incidence of similar behavior and results.

Again as a proportion of twins born and studied, this evidence is inadequate for genetic determinism and strong for identical developmental environments and for twins experiencing environments that are so stable that if they turn out differently from each other, it is more likely to be a surprise. So if we exclude genetic predispositions from developmental outcomes, then what makes some people flaunt socially appropriate actions, and some comply with all they require from society? This is then the propositional position that makes it impossible to always see psychology as a benevolent view or a deterministic way of the world and that, in fact, it could be that natural human conduct under a number of conditions is to be cruel, deceitful, abusive and prone to criminal behavior. Such morals are a privilege of a settled society in which everyone is economically equal, both in caste and class.

The Psychology of the Survivalist

There are those who see the end of civilization as a real possibility, especially in the USA, whether they support nuclear destruction (more likely today to be bio-warfare) or the fall of capitalism leading to societal instability and civil unrest. These individuals are also called survivalists. They store guns against the uncontrollable hordes that will roam the country and provide food for the possibility of shortages triggered by the economic meltdown in the event of a civil collapse. In the case of social collapse and lack of security rules, the survivors feel they have a fundamental right to defend themselves and their families. These groups are sometimes in dispute with current legal statutes implemented by federal agencies such as the FBI. Therefore, though in conflict with society, on the one hand, the survivalist's attitude is seen as a sincere effort to manage one's own destiny against future disasters on the other.

After all, insurance firms thrive on the assumption alone—and ironically, as shown by the collapse of many banks around the world in 2008/9, they will be the first to not survive an economic breakdown of capitalism. The most famous movies at the box office today are disaster films, those where earthquakes trigger the societal collapse of civilization, sun-flares, bio-warfare, alien invasion, and other catastrophes. The protagonists of these films are often resourceful survivors

DARK PSYCHOLOGY SECRETS AND MANIPULATION

who defend their kin from all-comers by violence. Why does the public find these people as appealing as heroes, and yet the actual survivors are vilified as status-quo public enemies? Judging by the popularity of these films, ordinary people realize that society's downfall is something that can happen or is simply imminent. So they look at these films as a kind of hope for another future that could be brought on by the collapse of their own daily world.

Psychology as Evolution

All individuals began as survivors in human history as hunter-gatherers wandering the land in search of easily accessible animals for food and warmth. As time goes on, we see these communities settling into agro-cultural settlements, establishing rules, regulations, representatives, and a moral code. These settled societies create art, music, and religion as they evolve and grow to compensate for a limited life within the constraints of the very society they have created. Land and property became important from these beginnings. The development includes the possession of goods and chattels. As time goes on, these settlements become villages, towns, and cities, gradually creating countries with borders. Survival is now the community and not the individual, as man's natural instincts from the beginning of time have been. Eventually, though, many of these cultures fade and crumble away.

Some for reasons unexplained, such as the Mayans and other cultures of South America. Most struggle as they grow into empires that rule the poor with a version of their own laws and religions. One thing history tells us all, however, is that civilizations vanish for all kinds of reasons. One thing all these cultures have in common was that they did not predict their own downfall. A European and American could not imagine the collapse of the EEC or the USA in today's world, but these new modern empires have their own "Capitalism" Achilles heel. While Karl Marx saw the evils of capitalism and its ultimate collapse, he could not have seen how the capitalist world would be hit to such an extent that wars over oil and gas would dominate the 21st century. Nevertheless, Marx would probably laugh with joy at the collapse of the financial system built on greed and debt around the planet's first nations in 2009.

Most of the failures can lead to mismanagement, but in reality, it was a lack of faith by ordinary individuals in the financial system that triggered a rush on funds and the inability to service crippling debt through high-interest rates and low return on investment. When people panic, they first look after themselves when they go into survival mode. It is time to conclude from these findings at this junction that social norms, rules, and morals for human beings are simply "not normal" and that society frequently imposes group actions based on what the powerful want over the powerless. That in fact, our norm is survivalist mentality, and that what society is actually attempting to do is regulate every human being's wild beast by teaching them from an early age to follow the laws, rules, and morality of the ruling community, typically the wealthy, who dominate our governments and institutions.

Therefore, should we denounce those who feel that society does not give them a reasonable deal, that they should simply take what they need to survive an often hostile world in which privilege depends on your education, family, or wealth? Does psychology itself need to come out of the closet and accept that static societies and laws are contrary to normal human behavior? Indeed, people hate society, but they experience some helplessness in trying to survive among the sheep because they are powerless against those who regulate law-making and morality. Is it any wonder then that often a single person takes it into their own hands to modify society or their own environment in order to live a more free self-controlled lifestyle away from the rigors of communities that inevitably break down and reinvent themselves as the new rich and wealthy take over again as we have all seen.

We saw China go from an empire dominated by depots to a military dictatorship ruled by the rich and powerful in the last century to turn itself into a communist stare of the 1950s where Marxism will decide a fair life for all and eventually to today's China as a capitalist-socialist state based on a political party that determines the lives of the powerless people, which actually fought for a fair life for all. Will another revolution take place in China in the future—at the moment, it seems impossible considering the turmoil of minorities forced to comply with the central rule in many parts of China. Not all empires will see the demise of their own!

How can psychology then answer this problem of human actions as a fundamental mechanism of survival that human beings are, in reality, inherently aggressive, cruel, and superior over those who are weaker than themselves? Mental hospital psychology is also used as social control officers—if you do not comply with society and its laws, then you must be insane—then you should be committed and monitored for the safety and good of others. On the other hand, psychology is seen as the liberating component of mental wellbeing—where we support those who are out of touch with culture to find their place and fit back into what the community considers normal behavior. Where is the solution for those who, without the intervention of the wealthy and the right to live a life they want to suit themselves, revolt against the world in which they live and want another form of existence?

Or wait for the tragedy that awaits all humans and a return to a dog-eat-dog life called survival—the real social standard—for the movies to come true!

How Is Dark Psychology Used Today?

Typically, sales or marketing systems are training programs that teach grim, unethical psychological, and persuasion techniques. Many of these programs use dark strategies to manufacture a brand or sell a product, not the consumer, for the sole purpose of serving themselves or their corporation. Many of these training programs persuade customers that it is okay to use those strategies because it is for the buyer's good. And of course, when they buy a product or service, their lives will be much easier. Who's using Dark Psychology and techniques of manipulation? Here's a list of individuals who seem to use these techniques the most.

- Narcissists—there is an exaggerated sense of self-worth in people who are genuinely narcissistic (meeting psychiatric diagnosis). To confirm their presumption of being superior, they need others. They have fantasies of being adored and worshipped. They use techniques of dark psychology, coercion, and unethical persuasion to keep up.
- Sociopaths—People who are genuinely sociopathic are also charming, articulate, yet impulsive (meeting psychiatric diagnosis). They use dark tactics to create a shallow relationship and then take advantage of people because of a lack of emotionality and the ability to feel guilt.
- Attorneys—some lawyers concentrate on winning their case so carefully that they turn to use dark manipulation techniques to get the result they seek.

- Politicians—to persuade people they are right and to get votes, some politicians use dark psychological strategies and dark persuasion tactics.
- Sales People—many salespeople are so focused on making a profit that they use dark strategies to convince others to purchase their product and persuade them.
- Leaders—some leaders use dark strategies to gain their subordinates' cooperation, greater effort, or better efficiency.
- Public Speakers—some speakers use dark strategies to raise the audience's emotional state, understanding that it leads to the back of the room selling more goods.
- Selfish People—this can be someone who, before others, has an agenda for himself. First, even at someone else's expense, they can use strategies to satisfy their own needs. They don't mind winning-losing results.

Yes, I know. Maybe I stepped on some toes. I also fall into this category as a speaker and a person who is interested in selling services. This is why I must remind myself that it needs me to resist manipulative and intimidating methods to work, compose, talk, and sell with character.

It's necessary to determine your purpose in order to distinguish between those dark motivation and persuasion techniques and those that are ethical. We have to ask ourselves whether the tactics we use are meant to assist the other person. It's all right for the sake of helping you, too, but if it's just for your gain, you can easily slip into dark and immoral practices. The aim should be to have a mutually beneficial or "win-win" result. However, for yourself and your assumption that the other individual would genuinely profit, you must be frank. An example of this is a salesperson who assumes everybody will profit from his product, and because of the purchase, life will be much easier for the consumer. A salesperson with this attitude will quickly fall into using dark strategies to drive the customer to purchase and use a mentality of "ends justifies the means." This opens the individual up to any and all methods to obtain the sale.

CHAPTER FOUR:

THE BASICS OF COVERT EMOTIONAL SITUATION AND MANIPULATION

What is Covert Manipulation?

There have undoubtedly been some ways of clandestine exploitation for thousands of years. Nevertheless, with the emergence of the Internet, new and structured hidden manipulation methods such as neuro-linguistic programming and pick-up artist techniques have increased to popularity in the last 15 years or so. It is possible that now more ordinary individuals are involved in covert deception than ever before.

Covert is a concealed, secret, or disguised adjective sense. Manipulation is the act of moving something around by hand or the act of manipulating, particularly to your own advantage, by artful, unfair, or insidious means. It is important to remember that not all covert manipulation strategies are essentially harmful, and not all people who use these methods are using them with the intent to hurt, control, or outsmart. However, the term covert manipulation is a precise descriptor for all of the methods listed below, regardless of the user's intent. For better or worse, without exposing a secret agenda, the goal is to subtly convince or steer others.

Covert emotional manipulation is the mechanism in which, without their awareness, one exercises power over the mind of the other only by conversing with the subconscious mind of the listener. The ultimate objective here is to alter the individual's perspective in question by influencing their thoughts and making them do things your way. The manipulator changes people's thinking habits, actions, emotions, and understanding of life on a subconscious level in this process. Covert stimulation does not require the closure of the eyes or some sort of rotating pendulum or odd hand movements, unlike traditional hypnotherapy sessions.

The use of propaganda, neuro-linguistic programming (NLP), pick-up artist techniques (PUA), obfuscation, subversive symbolism, etc., include unique covert exploitation techniques. Covert methods of persuasion are a form of mind control but more subtle than overt forms of brainwashing.

In practice, covert techniques of coercion can involve any of the following: using nonverbal cues to get others to like or agree with you, directing or directing conversations in such a way that only select information is exposed, encoding subliminal commands into speech or gestures, attempting to create a sometimes false sense of confidence or relationship with a target, making assumptions about the importance of a target, psychological motivations, wants, needs, or intelligence, not providing all the relevant facts and information, or even concealing the truth.

The instructions or recommendations given by the individual controlling the person being manipulated are more of a metaphor and are expressed in an indirect way, although they are also given explicitly in some instances. Stories are one of the covert deception techniques that can be used effectively to communicate the actual message and help it to be remembered with much greater probability. However, the initial step in covert manipulation is to create a bond with the listener. It's easy to do this with friends and family, but it's not that hard to do it with strangers either. All you have to do is use some compliments or laugh at their jokes to establish a degree of intimacy with your unidentified listener. You don't need to go too far to establish a bond with your listener.

You have to try to turn off the analytical mind of the listener after establishing a relationship with the person to be manipulated. It is nothing more than diverting the mind of the listener from its natural state of thought to an imagined state of thinking. You can always start by asking them questions like "What if..." or "Imagine this..." using some scenarios. This shuts off their rational minds immediately and allows their imagination to overtake their process of thinking. You can now render your irresistible commands and explain the stuff you want him/her to do after successfully getting the listener off his/her vital mindset. This method's success depends on a lot of things that you put into it. It depends on how you turn your mind from logical thought to creativity and the kind of statements you make to convince them well enough to carry out the job you are offering them. Salesmen, businessmen, therapists, and so on should practice this technique well. The listener essentially uses it to achieve positive results, but sometimes some evil-doers who have mastered this art will misuse it. It is an enjoyable practice that can also be taught to support others. So why not use this approach to enrich your relationships and business relationships and help others gain the same strength as well. I could also state the inference that I drew first before we discuss any of these particular approaches in more detail below. All covert methods of coercion are immoral, and this is why: when it helps us, we might be tempted to use covert strategies of persuasion, but we don't like the idea that without our knowledge, anyone is manipulating us secretly. You need to treat others how you want to be treated.

I began to learn these techniques individually to ensure that others would be more difficult to use against me. While some seem to be relatively benign, some, at first glance, seem deceptive. In fact, the urge to use persuasion techniques to my own advantage, especially in job interviews or adversarial situations, was strong while I was learning these techniques until I stopped considering whether doing so was ethical and truthful. Wisdom always asks, "Is it right?" If this was done to me, would I like it? Am I able without violence or purely for personal benefit and profit to use this knowledge? Even if the thought of someone secretly exploiting us is comfortable, it still doesn't make it right for them to do so. Covert methods of coercion, including those which are not intrinsically harmful to others, are still an effort without their knowledge to subvert someone's free will for personal gain or to fit an unstated agenda. Covert coercion means getting control over others, and the ability to use or abuse comes with that power.

Propaganda

Propaganda is secret mass-directed propaganda. Some methods include the use of dialectics (in order to influence the desired result, posing premeditated options to the public), misdirection, psychological engineering, and obfuscation of relevant evidence to distort public opinion, and so on. Non-verbal methods may also involve propaganda. In sporting events and military parades, the use of patriotic music is intentionally used to circumvent the rational faculty of the mind since music appeals to the right brain and emotions. Patriotic music is a valuable emotional instrument for a particular community or country for fostering coherence or mutual identity. Like other clandestine methods of deception, propaganda is usually immoral because it is subversive; an effort by nefarious or subconscious means to undermine the person's free will and the community.

Neuro-Linguistic Programming

Neuro-Linguistic Programming or NLP is a group of methods for use in communication, self-improvement, and behavior change popularized by the New Age and self-help movements. NLP ostensibly has two goals. You can use it to train the mind to conquer bad habits, to become more productive, and so on. If you find them useful, there is no ethical problem with using NLP techniques on your own.

NLP, however, duplicates a potent instrument of clandestine deception that can be used in the guise of persuasion tactics on others. NLP may involve the deliberate use of body language, such as mirroring (subtly imitating what the other person is doing such as crossing your legs when they do) to get others to like or agree with you, guiding or steering discussions to your advantage, anchoring (using specific words to guide the thinking processes of others), hiding subconscious suggestions within sentences or gestures, and trying to build trust or rapport with a target in order to unduly influence them.

In adversarial circumstances, knowing NLP is necessary in order for you to protect yourself and respond effectively if someone uses NLP on you. Some advocates of the NLP are not satisfied with using conventional debate and rhetorical skills; in order to make their arguments, they must focus on subterfuge. Defenses against subversive NLP include assertively pointing out when you are interrupted by others, not allowing you to answer a question, change the topic, or attempt to misdirect the conversation purposely. They don't have the advantage anymore when you call someone out on their underhandedness.

Pick Up Artist Technique

Pick up artistry, or PUA is a set of standard techniques of covert manipulation that rely on elements of pop psychology, game theory, and evolutionary psychology. The general purpose is to determine targets based on their physical features or sex rank and use covert coercion as a romantic partner to seduce them or protect them. A means to an end is the Pick Up Artist. The end game is advancing your own agenda, which can be anything from finding a good friend to as soon as possible during a random person into bed with you.

Pick Up Artist tactics may involve explicit displays of confidence or self-respect, having others trust you by rapidly developing relationships, subtly putting someone down (negging) to prove your own superior worth, touching someone to rapidly intensify a sexual experience, misdirecting to make a target believe that when it is, your objective is not sex, and so on. Depending on the intentions of the person using it, PUA may also involve outright lying.

A lot of PUA criticism comes from feminists who claim that predatory men who objectify women practice PUA. I will suggest that gender issues are unrelated to the ethical problems inherent in PUA, although some PUAs are definitely predatory. The majority of PUAs are men, I know, but some are women. It's not about so-called feminism or the rights of men. When used by both sexes, I argue that PUA can be similarly immoral. Any system of belief which promotes one gender's supremacy or superiority over the other is inherently unethical. Both sexes complement each other and complement each other. Egalitarianism is the natural product of neither gender seeking to violently control the opposite.

The ethical problems with PUA begin with egalitarianism's failure. You approach them from a place of superiority and shallow assessment of their relative worth rather than approaching anyone from a position of equality or human dignity. You think only about what you can learn from them or how you can exploit or influence them without tipping your hand by using your superior knowledge of psychology. The practice of the same involves secret control over others, even though you are not predatory in your use of PUA, and for less ethical pick-up artists, using the power at the expense of someone else.

I recognize that finding partners can be difficult and that there are a variety of superficial and social norms that are supposed to regulate the courting processes. That does not alter the fact that it is ethical and characteristic of a person of character, to be honest, and assertive about your wishes. It is not to use deceptive and hidden means to "game" others or lull them into a false sense of protection. The fact that PUA works are a sad reflection of humanity's current intellectual and moral situation.

Defending Techniques Against Covert Manipulation Tactics

Recognizing that they exist in the first place and that they are relatively common within society is the first safeguard against covert manipulation techniques. I do advocate a rational one, but I don't advocate a pessimistic or cynical worldview. Not everybody is truthful, assertive, or transparent, and many individuals, companies, and governments have their own secret agendas to drive.

In order to understand and identify them if they are ever used on you or if you see them used by the media, the second line of protection against covert exploitation is to research all the techniques available in depth. Even things that we don't agree with, we should think about everything. Some ways of covert exploitation, such as propaganda, are more or less lateral. You're not communicating with the root of the manipulation, but the forms it takes can still be recognized.

If you believe someone is misdirecting a conversation, attempting to convince you, invading your personal space, or steering you into something you don't want, assertive communication will help protect you against NLP or PUA techniques. Having clear personal boundaries that help protect you from predators and manipulators is also a good idea.

CHAPTER FIVE:

ANALYZING DARK PSYCHOLOGY

D ark Psychology believes that lacking any coherent rationality and all mankind has a reservoir of malevolent intent against others, ranging from minimally obtrusive and transient thoughts to pure psychopathic deviant actions. This is called the Spectrum of the Shadow. Dark Psychology calls the Dark Factor the mitigating factors that serve as accelerants and/or attractants to reach the Dark Singularity, and where the heinous acts of an individual fall on the Dark Spectrum.

Dark Psychology is a topic that has been grappled with by this author for fifteen years. Only recently, the meaning, theory, and psychology of this part of the human experience were eventually conceptualized. Dark Psychology includes all that makes us who we are in comparison to the dark side of ourselves. There is this proverbial disease in all cultures, all religions, and all humanity. There is a side lurking inside us from the moment we are born until the time of death, all that some have called evil and others have described as criminal, deviant, and pathological. A third psychological deception work is introduced by Dark Psychology, which approaches these practices differently from religious dogmas and theories in mainstream social sciences.

Dark Psychology believes that these same actions are committed by individuals and do so not for influence, wealth, sex, revenge, or any other known purpose. Without a target, they commit these horrid actions. Their ends, condensed, do not justify their means. For the purpose of doing so, there are persons who violate and kill others. This ability is inside all of us. The region that this author discusses is the possibility to damage others without cause, explanation, or intention. Dark Psychology believes that it is extremely complicated and much more challenging to describe this dark potential.

Dark Psychology believes that we all have the capacity for predator behaviors, and our emotions, feelings, and beliefs have access to this potential. As you can read in this manuscript, we all have this ability, but only a handful of us act upon it. At one time or another, both of us had thoughts and emotions of having to act in a brutal way. We all had thoughts of wanting to seriously hurt people without mercy. If you're frank with yourself, you'll have to admit that we've all had thoughts and emotions of wanting to commit heinous actions.

Despite the fact that we consider ourselves to be a compassionate race, we would like to assume that these thoughts and feelings are non-existent. Sadly, we all have these thoughts, and, thankfully, we never act upon them. Dark Psychology implies that there are individuals who have the same feelings, emotions, and experiences but act on them both in premeditated and impulsive ways. The clear distinction is that they work on these feelings, while others merely have brief thoughts and emotions to do so.

Dark Psychology believes that this type of predator is intentional and has some logical, objective-oriented motivation. Religion, philosophy, psychology, and other dogmas sought to characterize Dark Psychology cogently. It is true that most human conduct related to evil acts is purposeful and goal-oriented, but Dark Psychology assumes that there is an environment where it seems that intended behavior and goal-oriented motivation are nebulous. There is a spectrum in the victimization of Dark Psychology, ranging beyond any apparent rationality or intent from thoughts to pure psychopathic deviance. The Dark Spectrum, this continuum, helps to conceptualize the Dark Psychology theory.

Dark Psychology discusses the aspect of the human psyche or universal human condition that allows for and can even impel predatory actions. In certain examples, its lack of apparent logical motivation, its universality, and its lack of predictability are some features of this behavioral tendency. Dark Psychology believes this primary human condition to be distinct or an extension of evolution. Let us look at some of evolution's most basic tenets. Second, remember that we have evolved from other animals and are currently the paradigm of all animal life. Our frontal lobe allowed us to become creatures of the apex. Let us presume that being apex creatures does not entirely remove us from our animal instincts and predatory nature. If you adhere to evolution, assuming this is valid, and then you assume all-action relates to three primary instincts. The three main human drives are sex, aggression, and the instinctual desire to self-sustain. Evolution follows the concepts of survival of the species' fittest and reproduction. We act in a way to procreate and live, along with all other life forms. For the purposes of naming our territory, defending our territory, and eventually securing the right to procreate, violence takes place. It sounds logical, but it is no longer part of the human condition in the purest sense. Dark Psychology frequently believes that this dark side is unforeseeable. Unpredictable in the awareness of who acts on these risky urges, and even more unpredictable of the lengths others would go absolutely negated in their sense of mercy. Without cause or intent, there are people who rape, murder, torture, and rape. Dark Psychology speaks to these acts, without clearly specified motives, of behaving like a predator searching out human prey. As humans, to ourselves and any other living being, we are extremely dangerous. There are several explanations for this, and Dark Psychology seeks to examine certain hazardous components. The more readers are able to imagine Dark Psychology, the more prepared they are to decrease their risk of human predator victimization. It is important to have at least a limited understanding of Dark Psychology before continuing. This writer will go into depth about the most relevant principles as you progress through future manuscripts extending this build. The following are six concepts needed to fully understand Dark Psychology and the following:

1. A universal aspect of the human experience is Dark Psychology. Throughout history, this construct has had an impact. This facet of the human condition is preserved by all cultures, communities, and the people who live in them. This world of evil has the most compassionate people known, but they never act upon it and have lower rates of violent thoughts and feelings.

2. Dark Psychology is the study of the human condition as it relates to the feelings, emotions, and attitudes of people linked to this inherent tendency to manipulate others without specific, definable motives. Given that all action through modus operandi is purposeful, goal-oriented, and conceptualized, Dark Psychology puts forth the notion that the individual of the near era draws to the "black hole" of pristine bad, the less likely he/she has a motivational purpose. While this writer believes that pristine evil is never achieved since it is infinite, Dark Psychology assumes that there are those who come near.

3. Dark Psychology may be underestimated in its latent form due to its potential for misinterpretation as aberrant psychopathy. Examples of this latent propensity to expose itself as active, harmful activities are replete with history. The psychopath is described by modern psychiatry and psychology as a predator incapable of guilt for his actions. Dark Psychology posits that there is a spectrum of intensity without a rational intent or motive, ranging from thoughts and feelings of aggression to extreme victimization and violence.

4. The intensity of the Dark Psychology on this scale is not considered less or more horrific by victimization behavior but plots out a spectrum of inhumanity. Comparing Ted Bundy with Jeffrey Dahmer will be an easy example. In their deeds, both were extreme psychopaths and heinous. The difference is that Dahmer committed his atrocious murders when Ted Bundy murdered and sadistically induced suffering from pure psychopathic evil for his insane desire for companionship. On the Dark Spectrum, both will be stronger, but one, Jeffrey Dahmer, can be best understood by his desperate psychotic desire to be cherished.

5. Dark Psychology believes that all persons have the capacity for violence. In all humans, this ability is inherent, and different internal and external influences increase the risk of this potential manifesting into unpredictable behaviors. These behaviors are predatory in nature and can function without purpose at times. Dark Psychology believes that humans distort the predator-prey dynamic and lose all motives, assumed to be innate as part of the living organism of the world. Dark Psychology is a human phenomenon

only, and no other living being shares it. Among other living organisms, aggression and mayhem can exist, but humanity is the only species that has the ability to do so without intent.

6. An awareness of Dark Psychology's underlying causes and triggers would help allow society to identify, diagnose, and potentially decrease the dangers inherent in its effect. A two-fold beneficial function is to understand the principles of Dark Psychology. Accepting that we all have this evil ability helps those with this information to decrease the risk of its explosion. Second, recognizing the concepts of Dark Psychology relates to our initial evolutionary objective of fighting to live.

CHAPTER SIX:

THE ART OF MANIPULATION

One of the classic voices of intellectual dissent over the last decade, renowned critic and often MIT linguist Noam Chomsky, has compiled a list of the ten most popular and successful tactics resorted to by the "hidden agendas to create a media manipulation of the population.

The media has traditionally proved to be highly influential in influencing public opinion. Social movements, justified wars, tempered financial crisis, spurred on some other ideological currents, and provided the media's phenomenon as creators of truth within the collective consciousness were produced or destroyed thanks to media paraphernalia and propaganda.

Manipulation of the media is part of our everyday life. In a way that is comfortable for both of them, each occurrence is portrayed by the media. The misunderstanding of the truth generated in the audience by the media can lead to inappropriate human evaluation and conduct. Not only do the media have a social function, but they are also instruments for public temperature control. Manipulation of the media consists of how news is interpreted and relies on how individuals can interpret a mechanism and how they will respond to it. To different degrees, the media has a social role. They will talk about some problems and stay quiet about others. This is precisely what transforms them into a new kind of force.

In closed and oppressive countries, the media seeks to persuade the public that all government political and social acts should be recognized unconditionally. So they become part of the institutions of state control. The media is an intermediary between the government and the public in free and democratic societies. They should have a two-way flow of knowledge, and vice versa, from institutions to society. Media rivalry leads to a separation of news and information, also called media manipulation

But how can the most common techniques for interpreting these psychosocial devices, which we definitely engage in, be identified? Fortunately, the task of synthesizing and revealing these activities was given to Chomsky, some more prominent, some more sophisticated, but apparently all equally productive and, from a certain point of view, demeaning. Encouraging stupidity, encouraging a sense of shame, promoting diversion, or creating artificial problems, and then solving them magically are just some of these strategies.

There are measures to direct whole communities. There are several locations where Sylvain Timsit is named. Elsewhere a search ends with Les Cahiers Psychologie Politique, an interdisciplinary French-speaking journal, and Noam Chomsky is wrongly identified as the author.

It is not important to me if the tactics were or were not originally intended satirically. It is more critical that the methods appear relatively plain, logical, and empirically measurable—with a bit of regular distance. Such individuals may accept that with their fragmented range of themes and abridged knowledge bombardment, they not only rely on mass media.

The list is likely to be dismissed by someone who does this and sees the world from the viewpoint of a liberal pluralism according to which there is no power base, no hierarchy, and no law in society, but several distinct groups of actors who exercise their influence in a relatively balanced manner such that those ideas that correspond to the basic interests of the majority prevail.

Steering Attention

The tactic of diversion, which is to deflect public attention from issues and crucial improvements determined by the political and economic elites, is an integral aspect of social control. The mind becomes more docile and less critical through the flooding process, frequent distractions, and trivial details. In preventing mass interest in science, economics, psychology, neurobiology, and cybernetics, the strategy of diversion is also important.

The keyword here is "insignificance." Focus is a minimal resource. If a democratic society is to be structured such that there is a relatively little benefit when most others have to watch, the majority must be occupied with other items such that personal interests do not get in the way. Juvenal of the Roman Republic attested such a state of diversion under the term "bread and circuses."

Whoever respects the choice of themes in fellow people's TV, radio, newspaper, and conversations should inquire about the importance of specific themes for one's life or fellow people's lives by reflecting on the conditions of long-term joy in existence and then exploring how a sort of "inversion" of things can be uncovered by the relationship of employment time or attention investment to relevance for life.

There are exclusive deals in the store, tables of favorite teams, love affairs of the famous, the neighbor's child's name curiosity, medium-fat advantages compared to usual margarine, and so on vs. undermining civil rights, torture and threatened mass murder and secret wars by Western models, anchoring war, prejudice, and precariousness is normative

The Forced Problem, Reaction, And Solution Cycle

This strategy is often referred to as "Problem-reaction-solution." They establish a problem, a "situation," to induce a reaction in the audience so that the steps you can support become the standard. For instance:' let us escalate urban crime, or coordinate bloody attacks so that laws and policies that are detrimental to their rights are more appropriate to the public.' Or to trigger an economic crisis such that the public may support the annulment of social rights and the dismantling of public services as a necessary evil.

When social issues are concocted to provoke a particular need for population orientation, a solution in the ideological direction that is sought from the start is probable. In particular, serious crimes are committed when people's living conditions deteriorate.

Neoliberal proponents are very talented, as seen by the example of state finance, which was gradually undermined as public debts skyrocketed, and with the help of the media and business lobbies, the requisite fear was generated to introduce false solutions in the form of debt brakes. These inevitably lead to follow-up problems (financing bottlenecks, economic inflation, a further increase in government debt) that revitalize the old familiar idea of privatization as a resulting solution and significantly expand the sphere of control of massively concentrated private capital.

This implies privatization, deregulation, and a reduction in state spending. Resistance on the spending side to the trimming of the state comes from the beneficiaries of bureaucracy and subsidies. Emaciation or thinning would then presumably start with tax cuts on the tax side to help the hollow treasury dictate. As experience shows, this causes state deficits to rise. In the ongoing "Euro-crisis." this sort of tactic can be seen. Economic collapses are forced to push up mass unemployment by welfare cuts. The dismantling of the structure of collective bargaining fuels wage losses that contribute to corollary issues.

Naomi Klein illustrated many examples of this mechanism in her book "The Shock Doctrine," Whoever sees the knowledge advantage of the elites over their redirected populations particularly when the mass media acts as a "fourth branch" under resource scarcity and capital-connection factors and under a unanimous mindset, does not need much imagination to understand how quickly disasters, catastrophes, and other problems can be exacerbated and manipulated in many areas.

Gradation of Changes

To make an inappropriate measure acceptable, apply appropriate pressure gradually, drop by drop, over a couple of consecutive years. It is in such a way that during the 1980s and 1990s, new radical socio-economic conditions were imposed: the minimum state, privatization, poverty, flexibility, mass unemployment, wages that do not guarantee decent incomes, several reforms that would have given rise to a revolution if they had been implemented all at once.

As is obvious for light, pressure, noise, etc., their gradation often depends on understanding political processes of change. In the crisis from today to tomorrow, the economization of all fields of life cannot be implemented. Instead, if the cost-benefit, market, and management paradigm should be the all-pervasive social principle, it must be culturally sedimented through centuries by powerful institutions. On a smaller scale, these methods are also applied. In the case of the proposed cuts in the school and university sectors, an OECD publication advises that state grants be kept constant and not decreased because of the possibility of 'watchful political groups protesting.

Postponement of Changes

In order to gain public support at that time, another way to embrace an unpopular decision is to portray it as "painful and necessary" A potential sacrifice is easier to consider than an imminent sacrifice. First of all, because the measure is not immediately used; secondly, because the public, the people, still appear to naively believe that everything will improve tomorrow" and that the requisite sacrifice can be avoided. This gives the public more time to get used to the idea of transition and accept it without resignation when the time comes. If the planned worsening of conditions is on the agenda for a large part of the population, the supposed reasons for this should be set out early on. As long as the issue is not yet acute, civil society would be little impetus to investigate the claims. The built-up problem is made to appear as a familiar reality when it is imperative. In Germany, in times of permanent capitalist decline, demographic transition and global competitiveness have been placed in the spotlight, while pay, pension, and social cuts appear as "painful" but modern necessities.

Address In Children's Language

Most advertisements geared at the general public use dialogue, arguments, characters with particularly childish intonation, frequently targeting frailty, as if the audience were a creature of very young age or mentally disabled. The more you try to trick the listener, the more the adopted sound becomes childish. About why? If one goes to a person as if he or she were 12 years of age or less, then the other person appears, with some likelihood, to react or respond without much thought as a person 12 years of age or younger might, due to suggestive quality.

Vague messages are used to announce negative topics, where anything about what is said can be interpreted. For severe criticism, no attack surfaces are present. On the other hand, if the populace is addressed explicitly, a simple language that renounces pertinent information in a patronizing or solicitous compassionate tone pushes the collective counterpart into the position of the children. People are accustomed to corresponding to those role models triggered by environmental incentives at an early level. This technique may have the desired success in the form of unquestioning obedience and trustful acceptance, encouraging trust, in a highly conservative society with simple hierarchies and behavior patterns embedded.

Replace Feelings with Emotions

The puppet-masters do not want to trigger the thoughtful sides of people. They want feelings to stir up and enter the unconscious of people. That's why so many are full of emotional material in these messages. In logical thought processes, the point is to trigger a sort of short circuit." They use emotions to catch the general essence of the message, but not the details. This is another way of killing the critical thinking skills of people.

In evolutionary history, "Thinking" as a skill is new. The human spirit's foundation is an emotional heart that leads to judgmental powers at which gates justification watchmen literally deny their service. Inequality and unemployment are growing rapidly; the supreme motivations of humanity are "competitiveness" and population competition, and German tank deliveries to dictators are becoming the standard case for quenching rebellions.

Fostering Ignorance

Make sure that the public is unable to grasp the technology and tactics used to regulate and enslave. As weak and inadequate as possible, the standard of education provided to the lower social classes should be such that the difference of ignorance between the lower classes and the upper classes is and remains difficult for the lower classes to achieve.

Not knowing and not wanting to know may involve ignorance. Both situations can be closely intertwined. Not knowing can cause guilt. Different possibilities might then favor not wanting to know to escape embarrassment. One can remain totally away from societies and political power themes and keep the shame-filled knowledge of one's not-knowing out of the limelight, or one can ignore the value of knowledge and leap out of the way in formulas such as "nothing will change anyway!" and nothing can be done!" and the world runs that way!" which are ideal like curtains wherever the relaxed atmosphere will otherwise be.

There are forms of human activity used by the state and capitalist authorities to the detriment of the majority of the population. There is a significant gap between knowledge and the value of knowledge in economic relations. What does money mean? In the national economy, what is the role of wages and productivity? What do the conditions of distribution look like, and how have they developed? Who owns what and why? Why is there mass unemployment, and how does it impact a society's pecking order or balance of power? Strangely enough, these topics are hardly discussed or just in a non-controversial or fragmentary manner in school and commercial television—although the proposals linked to them still have the latest work in explaining incisive improvements in the macro-social range. "That costs jobs!" "We cannot afford this social state anymore!" and We need structural reforms!" are heard. "Competitiveness must be increased!" A democratic need here will be thorough information (at least if democracy should not be restricted to a blind motor act at the ballot box). However, by media brainwashing or through the job concentration, income competitiveness, and prestige anxieties, private enterprise lobbyism encourages systemic indifference of people, which narrows the attention to the close environment.

Propagating Mediocrity

Many fashions and patterns don't just come out of nowhere. There is almost always someone setting and encouraging them in motion. They do it to build tastes, desires, and views that are homogenized. The media are constantly marketing some fashions and trends. Much of them have to do with lifestyles that are trivial, pointless, even ludicrous. They tell people that what's in style is only behaving this way.

Standardized reality consists of living, eating, taking advantage of the possibilities of mass entertainment, and being equal in small items. People embrace the uniform fact and pass it on to their fellow individuals with responsibility.

Give Resistance A Bad Conscience

Make the person believe that he/she is the perpetrator of their own misfortune and make them question their intellect, expertise, or efforts. Thus, instead of rebelling against the economic system, the person devaluates and blames himself, which creates a depressed state, the object of which is to suppress action, and there is no revolution without action. Stephan Hessel, the renowned resistance fighter and co-author of the declaration on human rights, urged in a small book: "Be outraged!" He aimed at the discriminating, anti-social, and power-concentrated circumstances of our time that fundamentally threatened humanity and promoted a dedicated and educated standard of living that uses civil disobedience. To sabotage the assumptions of this kind of mentality, citizens must be given a bad conscience that paralyzes them in preserving conditions from the viewpoint of the functional elites. They are told they are deficient or even that human existence altogether is evil. The person is egotistical, selfish, and lazy. The individual who does not think that he is a "good person." In the varied TV entertainment, this implicit message can be heard, resounding in slogans such as "We have lived beyond our means" or in the devaluation and punishment of living conditions created by the social system followed by a public rabble against the socially disadvantaged. Instead of guiding this aversion towards the actual collective causal agents of misery, the environment generated here demoralizes large parts of the population as it steers the general aversion towards those fellow individuals who are bound to the social state. This atmosphere splits unity in that everyone is called to a bad knowledge and encouraged to withdraw so that they can be reliable and ready to accomplish in the immediate environment.

Knowing More About People Than They Themselves Know

Science has given us access to this kind of information about human biology and psychology over the last few decades. But most individuals still don't have this knowledge. The public is only ever reached by a tiny bit of data. The elites, meanwhile, have all this data and use it as they please. We can see once again how ignorance makes it easier for the forces that govern society. The aim of these media influence tactics is to turn the environment into whatever the most influential individuals want it to be. They obstruct the critical thinking skills and independence of everyone. But it's our duty to stop letting them manipulate us passively. We need to fail as much as we can.

Although all sorts of frequent barrages and commercial publicity magnets fix the population in confusion and distraction about social circumstances, according to the motto "knowledge is power," those who have everything to lose and substantial resources [do little to avoid this. Think tanks, for example, act here as organizations that, through studies suitable for functional elites and decision-makers, obtain millions from powerful capital interests and generate dominant expertise.

If you see the world as a causal network where an endless variety of causes and effects are linked together on the most different planes, institutions with enormous resources generate a fabulous social intervention-knowledge through comprehensive documentation and statistical analysis (big data and data mining), not radical academic theories.

CHAPTER SEVEN:

HYPNOSIS AND DARK PSYCHOLOGY

Self-Hypnosis

We sometimes need support in today's ever-changing world to get rid of patterns and ease our fears. We should turn to conventional techniques: physicians, government departments, and medicine over the counter. With therapists and psychologists, we can communicate. We can go on-it-alone, too. However, occasionally, when nothing we do seems to be helping our situation, we need a little support that's outside the box. It is time that self-hypnosis should be considered. It can function where all other methods have let us down.

A relative to hypnosis is self-hypnosis. It simply substitutes the client for a hypnotherapist or another trained individual. The hypnotist, in other words, is the client as well. Self-hypnosis, like hypnosis, is an instrument of consciousness and self-discovery. It is a medium by which anyone can reach the subconscious mind. Intentionally, you do so with the intent to shift the existing pattern of thinking maintained by the subconscious. You are beginning to lay the foundations for progress by doing so.

The object of self-hypnosis differs in accordance with the needs of the person. The fundamental function of this approach is to help a person reach into his or her subconscious deep down. You should retrain it to represent and accept what you want to achieve in doing so.

Certain traditional self-hypnosis uses include:

- To stop smoking
- Assisting with a diet
- Enhancing your overall self-image
- To help you conquer any fears
- Stopping things like procrastination
- Helping you address phobias
- To help you develop your memory

Stage Hypnosis

Hypnosis in stages is not hypnotherapy. Rather, the use of hypnosis for entertainment purposes is stage hypnosis. It is the art of the hypnotist in such shows to persuade the audience that hypnosis is a mystical and mysterious force. The greater the suspense and enchantment, the better the show will be. It is necessary to recognize that what the spectator sees is not a pure and mystical show of the forces of hypnosis. There is more going on than what you see or are told, like a good magic show.

The influence of stage subjects complying with commands attributable, not so much to hypnosis, but to a phenomenon called group or crowd anticipation, is a major factor seldom exposed. Psychologists know that when a person is in a crowd or large group of people, it is much easier to anticipate, control, and evaluate the actions of an individual. There is an influential force called stage conformity that significantly strengthens the apparent supernatural abilities of the stage hypnotist.

The stage subject(s) agrees to go along with the hypnotist by phase conformity, not because of the hypnosis, but because they do not want to let the audience down. They follow the hypnotist's orders to unbelievable ends; but not because they are in hypnosis and have no choice. But because they want to impress the public and escape the crowd's personal humiliation caused by not doing what is required of them. If they end up doing embarrassing stuff, like quacking like a duck, it does not matter; that's not the point.

The more they "quack," the stronger and louder, the more bizarre they are, the more hypnosis comes as mind control... The better they are for an artist, then. If they go with the show" instead of resisting the entertainer's orders, the audience would appreciate, approve and accept them more. Indeed, stage conformity may be more substantial than the hypnosis effect. I can testify to what the feeling is like after having been a stage subject on two distinct occasions.

In the stage show, does hypnosis play a part? Yes, but more to a degree only. Hypnosis is used in stage shows to help concentrate the mind. Using hypnosis to concentrate and clear the mindsets aside the multitude of conscious, frequently random thoughts for the moment. Again, a very powerful thing is a clear and concentrated mind. This, combined with phase conformity, does not really make the work of the hypnotist very difficult. They can focus a lot of their own energies simply on entertaining and livening up the show, you will find. The more they can persuade the hypnosis of the audience is mind control, the more the performance is interesting. And that is what is being presented; that is not what is happening.

Hypnosis is an activity that is very fun, calming, and mentally refreshing. It's like a relaxing mental break to take. It's easy to want to go along with the show as a stage subject because you feel that not doing so would end the fun hypnosis experience in which you are. It's not contemplating, grabbing, or hanging onto random ideas; the mind relaxes. This does not mean that the subject is asleep or has had their mind taken over in a coma. You know what's going on, and you are mindful of the sounds around you, maybe more so than in the usual consciousness of awakening. You know that you could wake up instantly if you really wanted to. But to what end? It is just as well to go with the experience if the hypnotist is respectful of your limits.

They either wake up or actually do not comply with the hypnotist's order when subjects are asked to do or say anything that goes against their legal, ethical, or religious beliefs. When in hypnosis, a topic does nothing that they would not usually do while they are awake, in the same sense and environment. With one stage topic which began to take off her clothes during the show, this came into question once, whilst the other subjects just went so far as that which is socially acceptable—pretending to "strip" but stopping well short of reaching the social norm. The hypnotist himself was very shocked and realized that the woman had to be stopped, which he did. It was not until he figured out after the show that her profession was that of a stripper.

Many hypnotherapists do not condone stage hypnosis or support it. Both stage hypnotists and hypnotherapists, there is a real break. The rationale for a stage hypnosis display works by presenting hypnosis as an unconscious state of sleep that lends itself to mind control. This is an erroneous view of hypnosis. It works to perpetuate the unfounded, socially held idea that hypnosis, which it isn't, is weird, strange, and bizarre. You're not falling unconscious; you're not in a trance; you're not controlling your mind. As a way to help others live a happier, healthier, and more fulfilling life, hypnotherapists prefer to use hypnosis. In addition, in their entertainment shows, stage hypnotists use hypnosis as the central prop. It is clear why a split exists.

Given the apparent discrepancies between the stage hypnotist and the hypnotherapist, by their application of hypnosis, the stage hypnotist unintentionally represents a percentage of humanity. Along with television portrayals, the stage show fuels the collective illusion that hypnosis is a strong and magical thing that taps the mind's strength. Putting the pieces together doesn't take long. I've done anything else; why not try the last resort of hypnosis? Oddly, I don't know how it works (fear of the unknown), but it doesn't matter to me... It could just work. That is the line of thought in the yellow pages that causes several telephone calls to the lists of hypnotherapists.

In an ideal world, in education, individuals will be taught what hypnosis is and how it works. Hypnosis's importance and advantages would be recognized, and there would be a more common position in culture for it. That is not the world today, however. When it comes to teaching the public about hypnosis, hypnotherapists have their job cut out for them. A long-term aim of the profession should be mass education.

This hypnotherapist, ironically, sees a lack of public education being introduced by hypnotherapists. Many brochures authored by hypnotherapists themselves appear to ignore the importance of hypnosis education. I assume that a number of hypnotherapists tend to retain "magical" and "mysterious" hypnosis because, unquestionably, this consistency will improve the clientele. At this point in time, to flat-out denounce stage hypnosis is rather premature.

Hypnotists of the stage area in a rare place to meet thousands of individuals who attend their shows literally. Stage hypnotists are encouraged to consider the high level of control they have that can be used to inform and educate individuals about the advantages of hypnosis and hypnotherapy. "Perhaps they will remind the audience at the end of the show of what was shown, "We had a wonderful time here tonight. I want each of you to realize that what you've seen is just a taste of what can be achieved by a determined mind. Aside from entertainment, hypnosis is just as important in helping to enhance the lives of people. To concentrate your mind on living a happier, healthier, and more fulfilling life, a hypnotherapist may use hypnosis.

What Is The Difference Between Self Hypnosis And Stage Hypnosis?

Hypnosis and self-hypnosis are respected types of therapy. These styles of hypnotherapy are used to accomplish a particular goal—one in which only the person who wishes to improve or needs a cure and the therapist are involved. The expectations set by the therapist and client are individualistic and designed to meet a specific need. The sessions and topics are confidential, personal, and carried out in a safe and secure atmosphere. If you are using self-hypnosis, what you need to do is understand why you are there. The main difference in the case of stage hypnosis is the stage. This is a success for the public. The hypnotist/magician has been paid to see what he or she can "make" someone do. Except maybe for their few minutes of fame, the "client" or stage prop is not there to accomplish any personal objective. To achieve his or her aims, the stage hypnotist may be deceptive and even exploitative. In addition, the whole technique requires more than a little deception and even self-delusion.

Types of Hypnosis

There are four major forms of hypnosis that are used to hypnotize another person or to hypnotize oneself in today's society. Standard hypnosis, Ericksonian hypnosis, NLP hypnosis, and self-hypnosis are the four primary forms of hypnosis. In terms of use and practice, each form of hypnosis varies. The primary common denominator among the four forms of hypnosis is that they all start to induce a hypnotic state with some form of hypnotic induction, such as fixed eye induction or counting backward.

Traditional Hypnosis

Traditional hypnosis is the most common type of hypnosis and is most commonly practiced with very little preparation and training because of the assumption that everyone can do it. It is often claimed that conventional hypnosis is the simplest type of hypnosis since it relies on easy suggestions and commands. This is the sort of hypnosis typically promoted with CDs and MP3s of hypnosis, along with tapes of hypnosis. While in a hypnotic state, traditional techniques of hypnosis communicate with the subconscious and use direct instructions and orders to control the attitudes, emotions, feelings, and actions of an individual. A suggestion about self-confidence or about quitting a bad habit like alcoholism or smoking may be examples of these orders. Since conventional hypnosis relies on suggestions and orders, it is often not seen as entirely successful for individuals who have logical and analytical thought processes. The conscious mind appears to interfere with the transmission of suggestions and instructions, questioning the messages and not allowing the subconscious to completely comprehend them. Traditional hypnosis is also the basis of stage hypnotism, which is common among partygoers and comedy club attendees in today's community.

Ericksonian Hypnosis

Ericksonian hypnosis is based on the concepts that Dr. Milton Erickson developed. For those wary of hypnosis, this type of hypnosis is especially excellent because it uses metaphors instead of only clear suggestions. Metaphors enable the brain to think creatively and come to conclusions that may not be drawn by using the more unilateral form of conventional hypnosis. In a more nuanced way than basic orders and suggestions, metaphors work by comparing and contrasting two objects.

In a more organic way than a direct suggestion, they often encourage the mind to wrap around an idea or a concept, which is why skeptics can often be hypnotized using this approach and not the conventional method. Isomorphic and interspersal metaphors are used for Ericksonian hypnosis. Isomorphic metaphors tell a moral tale that lets the unconscious mind draw a one-to-one connection between the story's morality and a situation or problem it is already acquainted with. Using embedded commands that confuse the conscious mind, interspersal metaphors allow the unconscious mind to process the metaphor's message.

Ericksonian hypnotherapy uses more subtle indirect suggestions. Indirect suggestions are much more difficult to ignore because the conscious mind often does not even consider them as suggestions, as they typically mask themselves as stories or metaphors. An example of an indirect suggestion is "and perhaps your eyes will grow tired as you listen to this story, and you will want to close them because people can, you know, experience a pleasant, deepening sense of comfort as they allow their eyes to close, and they relax deeply." Think of the following scenario: A child of five years of age brings a full glass of milk carefully to the dinner table. The parent of the child threatens in a stern voice, "don't drop that. The child looks up at the parent, stumbles, drops the bottle, and spills milk everywhere. "I told you not to drop that! You're so clumsy. You'll never learn!" yells the now furious parent.

As inadvertent as it might be, this is an instance of hypnosis. "The strong authoritative voice (the parent), having created an altered state (trance) by indirect suggestion ("don't drop that has given a clear post-hypnotic suggestion ("You're so clumsy. You're never going to learn"). In the future, this post-hypnotic suggestion by the parent may well stick to the order, sabotaging the progress of the infant.

NLP Hypnosis

To produce impressive results, NLP hypnosis blends neuro-linguistic programming (NLP) with hypnosis. NLP is a type of psychotherapy that links behavioral behaviors to neurological processes—basically, it links what we do to how we feel. Hypnosis is a way in which the subconscious is directly dealt with, sometimes bypassing the conscious mind; this suggests that the hypnotized individual becomes extremely suggestible and responsive to alteration of instructions and thinking.

In order to deal with concerns such as self-confidence, self-esteem, and general mental well-being, NLP hypnosis is used along with self-hypnosis. NLP hypnosis is also used to remove anxiety and phobias and overcome anxieties. This hypnosis approach is productive because it uses the same thinking pattern to reverse or get rid of the issue as fear or problem.

Maybe anchoring is the most popular NLP technique, and possibly everybody has encountered it at some point. Is there a song that activates emotions from the past when you hear it? If so, then the song has become an anchor for those emotions. You can anchor whatever you want to whatever emotions or mental states you want with NLP hypnosis. You can, for instance, anchor your ear with feelings of self-confidence.

You may easily touch your ear and reach those feelings of self-confidence and power if you feel nervous about something or are experiencing stage fright. It is important to select one that is precise, intermittent (otherwise desensitization would occur) when selecting an anchor (e.g., touching the top part of your right ear), and that it is anchored to a prompt and unique reaction (otherwise, the association would not occur).

The flash is a more sophisticated NLP hypnosis technique. In other words, it is used to dismantle a conditioned reaction, to eliminate a connection between two behaviors. For instance, when they are feeling hungry, many people like to have a cigarette. Over time, their minds will equate having a cigarette with being hungry, and whenever they are hungry, they will begin to crave a cigarette. To remove this connection, the flash can be used.

Another method in NLP hypnosis is called reception, and it is used to alter a person's conduct. The consequence is established (what the goal of the individual is), and then the subconscious is accessed and made to replace one set behavior with another, which is appropriate to the conscious, but would be more effective than the previous behavior to achieve the goal.

The appeal of NLP hypnosis is that to profit from it, you do not need to master the entire art. You may use it in isolation to enhance your life, even though you only understand one principle or technique of NLP hypnosis. The simplest technique to learn is anchoring, and we recommend that you try that first. When the methods are used either individually or all together, NLP hypnosis is considered to be one of the most powerful types of hypnosis.

Self-Hypnosis

As already mentioned, self-hypnosis is done by oneself in order to achieve a deep state of relaxation by using any of the above forms of hypnosis. Without a hypnotist or hypnotherapist, self-hypnosis helps the mind to relax and enter a hypnotic state. In the hypnosis session, suggestions and commands are then generated by yourself or by a CD or MP3 that directs you. Instead of guided hypnosis, many people now favor self-hypnosis because they do not trust others with their delicate and influential subconscious minds.

Subliminal Message

There are limiting values that are stopping you while you are trying to make a shift but don't seem to get results, and you need to remove them and instill new ones. It is only through the subconscious mind that this process will happen. The most effective, simple, productive, and pleasant technique that deals directly with the source—the subconscious mind—is subliminal messages.

Subliminal messages have been thoroughly studied and shown to be the best way to make fundamental improvements, time after time. Anyone can perform this technique, and its efficiency, performance, and ease of use make it highly common and the most studied. Subliminal messages have become popular among millions through a little-known strategy used by the elite.

Play Subliminal Messages While Sleeping

During sleep, subliminal messages will help you make great improvements and stick with them for the long term. With minimal effort, you can turn your 6–8 hours of sleep time into a personal growth seminar. You can easily spend 1/3 of your day by exposing your brain to subliminal messages in enhancing the problems you are struggling with and programming your subconscious mind to get rid of harmful patterns of thought.

Subliminal signals are going to drive you further than ever! This way, you can use subliminal messages as the most influential people do. When you read the daily news online,

DARK PSYCHOLOGY SECRETS AND MANIPULATION

you can gradually build your confidence; you will grow spectacular social skills and learn to easily make new friendships when checking out your favorite pie recipes. When checking your email box, you can program yourself to feel happy; when liking posts on Facebook, you can build optimistic money paradigms.

You'll begin to feel the tension leave your mind and body with just a few moments of listening. You will find yourself lost in a profound sense of pure comfort and worry-freeness. In addition to all the beautiful objectives you can accomplish by using subliminal messages, with a positive spirit, you can also boost your sleep and wake up energetic, new, and vibrant. Here at the Vortex Performance audio library, you will find life-changing subliminal messages.

Watch Subliminal Flashes On Your Computer Screen
Subliminal messages can, as you know, be conveyed by audio, but also visually. The subliminal visual signals will appear on your computer screen as short flashes. You can spend only a few minutes a day using this system of subliminal messages. There are optimistic affirmations in the subliminal messages, and being exposed to them over and over will create a new neural network in your brain. The essence of all this is that you can be the person that you want to be.

The subliminal claims will become your reality, and you can finally let yourself become the strong person you always wanted to be. You can quickly manifest the affirmations and make them come true with those subliminal messages in the form of flashes. Setting up subliminal messages on your PC is really simple; watch this video, scroll down and press the 'live demo' button to see how it's done.

Play MP3 Subliminal Messages During Daytime

While it is advised before or during sleep to listen to subliminal messages, there are other successful ways to use subliminal during the day when the mind is in a receptive state.

When we are alive, can the subconscious mind consume the subliminal signals and be programmed? Completely! Absolutely! The brain works with beta waves during the waking time, but fresh knowledge can still enter the subconscious mind. All the time, fresh knowledge enters the subconscious. The only difference is that we can effectively interact with the subconscious mind during the processing of alpha and theta waves. We don't have to interact consciously with the subconscious throughout the day; we can simply let it unconsciously consume the subliminal messages.

Another highly productive way to use subliminal messages during the day is to play subliminal MP3 meditations in the background, in addition to subliminal flashes. You can cook, clean the house, take a relaxing bath or watch a TV show of your choosing.

CHAPTER EIGHT:

THE ART OF PERSUASION AND DARK PSYCHOLOGY

What Is Persuasion?

What comes to mind when you are thinking about persuasion? Some people may think of promotional ads urging viewers to purchase a specific product, while others may think of a political candidate seeking to persuade voters to pick his or her name on the ballot box. In everyday life, persuasion is a dominant force and significantly influences society as a whole. Politics, legal rulings, mass media, news, and advertisement are all influenced and impact us in turn by the power of persuasion.

We like to think even that we are resistant to persuasion. We have a natural ability to see beyond the sales pitch, grasp the facts in a case, and come to our own conclusions. In some instances, this may be true, but persuasion is not just a pushy salesman trying to sell you a car or a commercial on television, tempting you to buy the latest and greatest product. Persuasion can be subtle, and a number of factors can depend on how we respond to such influences.

Negative examples are always the first ones to come to mind when we think of persuasion, but persuasion can also be used as a positive power. Great examples of persuasion used to change the lives of people are public service ads that encourage people to recycle or stop smoking.

And what is persuasion exactly? According to Perloff (2003), persuasion can be characterized as a symbolic process in which communicators try to convince other people to change their attitudes or behaviors regarding an issue through the transmission of a message in an atmosphere of free choice."

In this definition of persuasion, the main elements are:

- Persuasion is symbolic, using phrases, pictures, noises, etc.
- A conscious effort to manipulate others is involved.
- Self-persuasion is important. People are not coerced; they're free to choose instead.

There can be a range of methods of transmitting convincing messages, including verbally and nonverbally, through television, radio, internet, or face-to-face contact.

How Does Persuasion Differ Today?

Although the art and science of persuasion have been of interest since the time of the Ancient Greeks, there are major variations in how persuasion occurs today and how it occurred in the past. Richard M. Perloff outlines in his book The Dynamics of Persuasion: Communication and Attitudes in the 21st Century the five main ways in which current persuasion varies from the past:

The amount of compelling messages has risen enormously. Think for a moment about how many commercials on a regular basis you see. According to different reports, the number of ads the average U.S. adult is subjected to per day varies from about 300 to over 3,000. Persuasive dialogue moves much more easily. Television, radio, and the Internet, all help to very rapidly, spread convincing messages.

Big business is persuasion. In addition to businesses that are solely for convincing purposes in the industry (such as advertising firms, marketing companies, public relations companies) and many other companies, persuasion to sell products and services relies on persuasion. Much more subtle is contemporary influence. Of course, there are plenty of commercials that use very obvious persuasion tactics, but many messages are much more subtle. For example, in order to achieve the projected lifestyle, advertisers often carefully craft very detailed photos designed to urge audiences to purchase goods or services. Persuasion is more dynamic. Consumers are more complex and have more options, so when it comes to choosing their compelling medium and message, marketers have to be savvier.

Modern Persuasion

Pratkanis & Aronson (1991) argue convincingly that Western societies favor persuasion even more than other cultures do. Marriages are not arranged; they are left to each couple's convincing strategies. The processing of customer preferences and choices is left to the advertiser, unlike communist countries that regulate trade. Arguments are not resolved by the leaders of the clan or religious officials but by the lawyers' wrangling. Due to their ability, rulers are not royally born or selected but emerge through one of the largest rituals of persuasion of all the election campaigns. Almost always, the nominee who has both good looks and a compelling personality wins.

The ancient Greeks had an approach to persuasion that was more grounded. To help him learn to argue, a Greek citizen might employ a Sophist. Sophists were itinerant professors and authors committed to knowledge—you could suggest they were ancient world graduate students. The Sophists believed that persuasion was a valuable method for finding the facts.

They thought it would expose bad ideas to the process of arguing and discussing and encourage the good ones to be exposed. A sophist didn't care what side of a problem he was talking about. In fact, in the middle of a debate, Sophists would often turn sides. Their stated purpose was a logical argument that revealed the facts. They believed in good ideas for the free market.

Does our world sound like that? No—we rely even more on the use of persuasive and enforcement strategies than the ancients did. But does it take the form of logical argument and discussion to take the new approach to persuasion? Scarcely. "Through the manipulation of symbols and of our most basic human emotions through the manipulation of symbols and of our most basic human emotions.

Since the ability to convince and resist persuasion is directly linked to the success of one's life, you would assume that the subject would be taught in school. As well as learning the letters of the alphabet, or the Ten Commandments, or how to do CPR, you'd think people would know their persuasion techniques. But how many of us can recite ten convincing principles? How many of us will analyze a situation and pick the best persuasive instrument for the job at hand? How many of us are even conscious of the thousands of times that someone else affects us each day? Do this: take a look at your cabinet for medication, your pantry, or your garage. Each thing you see is a trophy of war, reflecting the triumph of some companies over their competitors. They persuaded you, for some reason—or maybe for no reason at all—to exchange your hard-earned cash for their commodity. Exactly how did they do that? Don't make a mistake. There are legions of agents of power employed in our culture. By getting you to think things and do things that they want you to think and do, they flourish—they live at the pinnacles of influence.

Many individuals are either ignorant of these factors, or when they are, greatly overestimate the amount of liberty they have to make up their own minds. But the good agent of influence knows that the answer to his technique would be as reliable as the springing of a mousetrap if he can handle the situation and choose the correct procedure.

Persuasion Techniques

The ultimate purpose of persuasion is to encourage the target to internalize the convincing claim and accept this new attitude as part of their core value system. The following are only a couple of the techniques of highly efficient persuasion. The use of incentives, penalties, positive or negative expertise, and many more are other approaches.

Establish a Need

One form of persuasion is to build a need or to appeal to a previously established need. This method of persuasion appeals to the basic needs for shelter, affection, self-esteem, and self-actualization of a person. This technique is also used by advertisers to sell their goods. Consider, for instance, how many ads say that in order to be happy, healthy, respected, or appreciated, people need to buy a specific product.

Appeal to Social Needs

The need to be famous, prestigious, or similar to others appeals to another very successful convincing process. Television advertisements provide many examples of this kind of persuasion, where audiences are persuaded to buy things so that they can be like someone else or be like a person who is well-known or admired. Television commercials are a huge source of persuasion publicity, provided that some reports say that the average American watches television between 1,500 and 2,000 hours per year.

Using Loaded Pictures and Words

Persuasion often sometimes makes use of words and pictures that are loaded. Advertisers are well aware of the power of positive words, which is why phrases such as' New and Improved' or All Natural' are used by so many advertisers.

Get Your Foot in the Door

The "foot-in-the-door" strategy is recognized as another effective method in getting people to comply with a request. This technique of persuasion includes getting an individual to agree to a small request, such as asking them to buy a small item, followed by making a much larger request. The applicant already has their "foot in the door" by getting the individual to consent to the small initial favor, making the person more likely to comply with the larger request. A neighbor asks you, for instance, to babysit her two kids for an hour or two. Once you consent to the smaller offer, she then asks if you can only babysit the twins for the rest of the day.

Since you have agreed to the smaller request already, you will feel a sense of responsibility to agree to the larger request as well. This is a perfect example of what psychologists refer to as the dedication law, and advertisers also use this technique to persuade customers to purchase goods and services.

Go Big and then Small

The opposite of the foot-in-the-door technique is this method. By making a big, sometimes unrealistic request, a salesperson can start. By refusing, the individual responds, figuratively slamming the door on the deal. By having a much smaller offer, which sometimes comes off as conciliatory, the salesperson reacts. Individuals also feel compelled to respond to such offers. Since they rejected the initial request, individuals often feel obligated to assist the salesperson by approving the smaller request.

Using The Power Of Reciprocity

You undoubtedly have an almost overwhelming responsibility to return the favor in kind when individuals do you a favor. This is known as the reciprocity rule, a social responsibility to do something for someone else when they have done something for you first. By making it seem like they are doing you a favor, including "extras" or discounts, advertisers could use this pattern, forcing individuals to accept the deal and make a purchase.

Build An Anchor Point For Your Negotiations

A subtle cognitive bias is the anchoring bias that can have a strong effect on negotiations and decisions. The first bid appears to become an anchoring point for all subsequent discussions while attempting to arrive at a decision. So if you're trying to negotiate a pay raise, being the first person to propose a number will help impact the potential negotiations in your favor, particularly if that number is a bit high. That first number will become a point of departure. Although you may not get that number, starting high could lead to your employer's higher bid.

Limit Your Availability

In his best-selling 1984 book Influence: The Psychology of Persuasion, Psychologist Robert Cialdini is famous for the six concepts of influence he first described. One of the main concepts he defined is known as scarcity or restriction of something's availability. When they are scarce or reduced, Cialdini suggests that items become more desirable. If they hear that it is the last one or that the sale will end soon, people are more likely to purchase something. For instance, an artist could only make a limited run of a specific print. Because there are only a few prints left for sale until they are gone, people may be more likely to make a purchase.

Spend Time Taking Note Of Persuasive Messages
The above examples are only a few of the many methods of persuasion mentioned by social psychologists. In your everyday practice, look for examples of convincing. An interesting experiment is to watch a random TV show for half an hour and remember any instance of convincing ads. The sheer quantity of persuasive techniques used in such a short period of time might surprise you.

CHAPTER NINE:

THE ART OF DECEPTION AND DARK PSYCHOLOGY

What Is Deception?

Deception refers to the act of getting another to believe something that is untrue—big or small, cruel or kind. With different research demonstrating that the average person lies many times a day, even the most truthful individuals practice deceit. Some of those lies are huge ("I've never cheated on you!"), but more often, they are little white lies ("That dress looks good,") that are employed to prevent awkward circumstances or spare the feelings of another.

Deception is not always an act that is outward-facing. There are also the lies people tell themselves for reasons ranging from healthy preservation of self-esteem to extreme delusions beyond their control. Although lying to oneself is commonly viewed as negative, some experts argue that there are some kinds of self-deception that can positively impact overall well-being, such as thinking one can achieve a challenging objective even though there is evidence to the contrary.

For a long time, researchers have been searching for ways to definitively detect when someone is lying. The polygraph test, one of the most popular, has long been controversial, and research suggests that polygraphs or other widely used methods of detection of lies do not reliably measure those with such psychological conditions as Antisocial Personality Disorder.

Do lies have a functional purpose in life? In spite of what your parents told you, psychologists agree that revealing the whole truth may potentially set you back in certain circumstances. Not only that, but studies show that it's more common to lie than you would think. Research led by Dr. Bella DePaulo has found that people lie twice a day on average. The average person tells a lie to roughly one out of every three individuals they speak to one-on-one over the course of a week. Like it or not, we've built a world where you don't always get ahead by telling the truth. In reality, lies can make it easier to get along with the people around you, proven by research findings showing that individuals routinely lie for the benefit of others.

DePaulo discovered that it is very normal for individuals to lie for no reason other than to make others better. Women do this even more frequently than men, who have been found to lie more to boost their own reputations. A conversation between two men, in fact, usually includes eight times as many lies about themselves as about anything else.

The lies help even individuals who are told little white lies. A study published in the Journal of Market Research's April 2012 edition found that individuals who were lied to were subsequently viewed with more compassion and generosity. It's not that we don't know we're lying; we know, and we feel guilty enough times to let it affect our actions in the future.

The ease with which we can deceive each other and the popularity of lying makes dishonesty an aspect of our culture that should not be overlooked and will not soon disappear. However, do most individuals tell lies to succeed? The personal benefit doesn't seem to be the reason behind most lies, and in your professional and personal life, repetitive lies will definitely come back to haunt you.

Alternatively, proof overwhelmingly shows that we lie more about others and for the sake of everyone getting along—rather than getting ahead.

No one likes being misled, and it can become a big scandal when public figures are caught in a lie. But while many individuals pride themselves on their scrupulous integrity and strive to distinguish themselves from others who are more comfortable with falsehoods, for a variety of reasons, the fact is that everyone lies. In fact, some experts say that for maintaining a stable, functioning community, a certain amount of deception might be appropriate. Formerly the domain of ethicists and theologians was the systematic study of deceit, but more recently, psychologists have turned their attention to why people lie and the circumstances that make them more likely to do so.

Case Research studies

Are meat eaters more egotistical than vegetarians? Do chaotic circumstances facilitate stereotyping? Will we feel smarter when prizes are won by people close to us? The study of influential Dutch psychologist Diederik Stapel has recently answered these and other interesting questions. Stapel published over 130 research papers just 15 years after earning his Ph.D. with honors in 1997, received a career trajectory award from the Society of Experimental Social Psychology, and rose to become dean of the faculty at his university. In 2011, however, it began to dawn on his students that his research had only one issue: he was making up the data.

For no less than 55 of his papers, an investigation by his university has so far revealed that Stapel fabricated the results. This has prompted many influential scientific journals to issue retractions, including Science. Since then, Stapel has publicly apologized to his employers and students. A memoir,

Derailed, in which he recounted his personal descent into scientific misconduct, was also published. It has been described by fellow psychologists as "priceless and revealing," particularly its "unexpectedly beautiful" final chapter, although they also note that it is riddled with plagiarized lines from Raymond Carver and James Joyce's writings.

How did a psychologist so globally know, a man whose work was featured in The New York Times and Again, get caught up in such a web of deception? Most of us would like to suppose that in a scientific field such as psychology, the emergence of fraud is a fluke, the work of a rogue researcher on the fringes of the discipline. Yet, the real roots of the issue are profound and pervasive. The issue goes to the heart of contemporary psychology: many psychological researchers have embraced deceit as a necessary evil in the pursuit of reality.

Consider the account that follows

At a big urban research university, Beth is a sophomore psychology student. She volunteered as a participant for a study exploring the disparity between contact that takes place online and in-person as a prerequisite for her introductory psychology course. She was led to a small cubicle by a pair of graduate students dressed in white lab coats, where she read a brief article on the history of medicine and discussed it in a chat room with someone she was told was another student. When her chat partner expressed disbelief about an African American researcher's achievements, she was shocked, but she shrugged off the remark and completed her task. A third graduate student then took her to another room and told her that, in fact, this was a thesis on contemporary racism. Beth then recalled casually making negative comments about another student, who was also African American, to the other graduate students. The graduate debriefing student gave her some paperwork to read about the procedures and goals of the study and sent her on her way. Beth felt remorse and disappointment, reflecting upon her experience. Why was she deceived?

In the search for reality, there is something fundamentally problematic about using deceit. But deception has played a prominent—and many would argue integral—role for well over a century in psychological science. A participant who enrolls in a research study is sometimes confused about its specific intent, the answers researchers are actually tracking, and the true identity of fellow "subjects." Participants are not even told in some instances that they are participating in a research study. In psychological science, how did the tradition of deception grow, where does it stand today, and what are the issues with its continued use?

For deception, different rationales can be given. One is that everything around us is deceitful, permeating fields like ads and politics. There is no need to hold psychological researchers to a higher standard, proponents argue. Another is the statement that there is no actual harm to subjects. Feelings can be damaged, but no one is asked to donate blood or lose a limb under false pretenses. The most common argument is that without deception, much analysis will be difficult. Much as physicians monitor respiratory rates without calling attention to a patient's breathing, while subjects are unaware, psychologists need to observe behavior. As the only way to replicate natural behavior in the laboratory setting, deceit is rationalized.

Deception became a hallmark of psychological science during the first two-thirds of the 20th century. Until 1950, only about 10 percent of papers in social science journals involved misleading techniques, according to a new history of deception in social psychology. By the 1970s, the use of deception had reached over 50 percent, and the number reached two-thirds of the studies in some papers. This suggests that participants in social psychology studies had a greater than 50-50 chance of getting the facts hidden from them being told things that were not real or being exploited in clandestine ways, at least those that survived the peer review process and made it to print.

Proponents of deceit claim that in order to expose big secrets, they use little lies. Many subjects voice no objection, and the procedure is readily supplied with sophisticated ethical defenses. Deception can be scrupulously avoided in an ideal world, perhaps, but ours is not perfect, so advocates argue that compromises must be made. Of course, they admit, researchers can, whenever possible, do their best to prevent manipulation, using it only as a last resort. In certain cases, alternative methodologies, which do not require it, may be possible to create. However, in the end, deceit is an important instrument in the search for information.

The American Psychological Association provides clear support to the claim that scientific advancement involves dishonesty. "The view that the ends justify the means apparent in the Psychologists' Ethical Principles and Code of Conduct of the APA, which reads as follows: "Psychologists do not conduct a study involving deception unless they have decided that the use of deceptive techniques is justified by the substantial potential research, educational or applied benefit of the study and the effective non-deceptive alter the value of the study

Psychology is the nation's second most popular undergraduate major, totaling about 90,000 students since the mid-2000s. Permissive attitudes towards deceit permeate most introductory courses in psychology. Students are also expected to serve as participants in many psychological experiments, such as the one mentioned above, in order to obtain a passing grade. Many students have no idea at first that they may be fooled by scholars, teachers, and fellow students. As the course progresses, they discover that many of the best-known psychological studies of the 20th century were based on deceptions of one sort or another. Students can be persuaded by the end of the semester that deceit is a valid technique.

Suppose an undergraduate psychology student goes home during a school break to visit her family. A friend asks a question during the visit that the student would prefer not to answer for one reason or another truthfully. Having been advised that deceit is always justified for the sake of higher ends by textbook writers and professors, could such a student be more likely to withhold information, provide misleading information, or misrepresent the truth? After all, if deceit in the pursuit of information is allowed in scientific experiments, why should it be impermissible in the sense of daily relationships? In a white lie, where is the harm?

Consider the relationship between a salesman of a used car and a client. Should the buyer believe everything the salesman says blindly? Not, of course. But in the fields of science and higher learning, does this same idea apply? The motto of the marketplace may be "Buyer beware," but Let research subjects beware" is not the sign we want to see hanging over the door of the laboratory. In research, the practice of deception undermines the relationship between science and the society that it studies. The more suspicious subjects consider jobs, the less scientifically important their presence becomes. The more we hope to be fooled, the less honest our answers represent what we really think and feel.

Yet perhaps the most important thing at stake is not the impact of deceit on science. The fundamental issue is fundamentally the ethos of our entire society. Scientists are trusted highly. When such trusted figures turn out to be engaged in fraud repeatedly, confidence in them and maybe in everyone else eventually decreases. The idea that we should expect authenticity from those entrusted with the pursuit of truth is compromised by deceit in psychological study.

Deception may be habit-forming, like truth-telling. The more often we indulge in dishonesty, the simpler it becomes and more normal. Should we really believe that deception practice can be safely contained in the laboratory? For the sake of a seriously mistaken conception of scientific advancement, are we willing to compromise the quality of truthfulness and the habit of honesty? We must agree that scientifically sanctioned deception is fundamentally incompatible with the pursuit of truth.

CHAPTER TEN:

PROTECTING YOURSELF FROM EMOTIONAL MANIPULATION

Once in a while—men as well as women—we all enjoy chasing the other sex. As long as we are honest about it and keep in mind that it has nothing to do with love, it is fun and a good sport. About why? Because manipulation is pursued and love cannot be manipulated—we don't find love; we find love. We should, therefore, treat a love relationship as sacred ground.

Unfortunately, so many people believe in deception—in relationships as well as in industry. In my early twenties, I read something that got stuck for good in my subconsciousness: if you can align yourself with the cosmos, success comes easy. For this subject, what does that mean? This implies that tampering is futile at the end of the day. Manipulations may help to bring about a short-term benefit but will inevitably lead to repercussions in the long run because the cosmos oppose manipulations. But if we go with the cosmic flow instead, we will gravitate more or less effortlessly toward our goal. O nice to be true? In a cosmic game, each of us plays a role. In the scheme of things, we just have to know our role and let it play out. That is why Jesus said that as light as a feather in his cross. This means, of course, surrendering a lot of wishes and aspirations that are not part of our cameo, but our celestial intent typically turns out to be much more grandiose than our little, selfish ambitions.

Having said that, we also need to defend ourselves and those close to us from childish manipulation by other people. Do not take this lightly; it is hard to exploit emotionally and can leave deep wounds on the heart and souls of people. And it's really difficult to get out once you're in a tricky situation. But don't take this affair too seriously, we do a lot of things subconsciously, and maybe your wife doesn't even know she's manipulating you. There will always be people trying to shake your faith—people trying to instill within you seeds of self-doubt. In order to trick you into thinking that their views are a valid reality, these people will do their best. They're going to tell you that everyone thinks you're rude, nuts, or not good enough in the whole world. Then they're going to tell you how worried they are about you, about how you live your life, spend your money, raise your children, go on and on.

Your life will be destroyed if you do not change exactly the way they want you to change. This is what they would like you to believe. The reality is that you don't want to help these people. They want you to be monitored. They want to improve you, not to make your life easier, but to affirm their lives and prevent you from outgrowing them. Don't be puzzled. There are no manipulative people worried about your interests. They have their interests worried. Once you let manipulative people in your life, they can be extremely hard to get rid of. The key is having enough confidence in yourself to give manipulative people the boot as soon as you spot them. Here are some strategies to eliminate people from your life who are manipulative:

Don't Fall into Their Trap

Most of us come across situations when others try to control our emotions, perception, or behavior and take advantage for their own benefit. In one such as you fail to realize the real motive. The person controls you psychologically, and you get into the trap. This emotional manipulation sometimes costs you a lot when you make some important decisions under the influence of another person and realize it later when it is too late.

When a relationship sounds too good to be true, you must be aware. They shower love, praise, appreciation, compliments, and affection on you. You feel as if you are living your dream where everything seems perfect. They give you no reasons to complain. You simply find no faults in them. Even if something goes wrong, they may start crying or feeling sorry. You may even become the victim of intense sex and get the feeling of a fairy tale love.

It is the result when the relationship actually started off with love bombing, and all of a sudden, you start feeling neglected. You get appreciation, gifts, and praise, but only rarely. You feel as if you are losing your grip, or they have someone else in their life. The moment you make up your mind to move on, you get another gift from them. You find it difficult to make up your mind. In one such situation, they try to get control over you. To your amazement, in most cases, it works. You get even closer to them.

After sporadic reinforcement, people mostly succeed in controlling their victims. When you fight back or demand an explanation, they may stop behaving in the same manner. The reason is that they actually get complete control over you now, so they say goodbye to the sporadic reinforcement. They do not need it anymore. Manipulators have many different faces, and they may use many different ways to get things done in the same manner. The person may commit and later deny it so that you start doubting your own perception. When you try hard to make them aware of their promise, they make you feel guilty. They may use superficial sympathy and burst into crocodile tears. You end up trusting them eventually and even doubt whether you heard right. You cannot trust smiling faces that appear confident and powerful. Manipulative people always have a self-serving bias, and they hardly care for the other person's feelings. They have a motive to seek out people who validate them and make them feel even superior.

Steer Clear Whenever Possible

The behavior of a manipulator usually varies depending on the situation they are in. For instance, a manipulator could speak rudely to one person and act politely towards another the next moment. When you notice such extremes frequently in an individual, it would be advisable to stay away from them. Don't interact with this individual unless you really have to. This will protect you from being a victim of manipulation.

One way to detect a manipulator is to see if a person acts with different faces in front of other people and in different situations. While all of us have a degree of this type of social differentiation, some psychological manipulators tend to habitually dwell in extremes, being highly polite to one individual and completely rude to another—or totally helpless one moment and fiercely aggressive the next. When you observe this type of behavior from an individual on a regular basis, keep a healthy distance, and avoid engaging with the person unless you absolutely have to. As mentioned earlier, the reasons for chronic psychological manipulation are complex and deep-seated. It is not your job to change or save them.

There are certain situations where you can't exit a relationship completely—most commonly if this person is a parent or a member of your extended family. Unless the person is causing significant harm or psychological damage, you probably can't go cold turkey. First, you need to fully recognize this person for who they are and alter your expectations of the relationship accordingly. If they were previously someone you wanted validation from, then you'll have to stop seeking their validation. If they were someone you got advice from, recognize that their advice isn't something you need in your life. If they continue to offer it, you can thank them for it and then silently discard it.

Be as subtle as you can when setting these boundaries, and don't tell the other person that you are setting them. Creating this change on your end is going to require some energy, and when you anger the other person in the process, you'll have to handle their reaction on top of that.

Knowing that this will drain your energy a bit, set boundaries around your time with this person. If you have been hanging out with your controlling mother-in-law every Saturday, cut it down to once a month and schedule something later that day so that your hangout has a definite end time.

Call Them Out On Their Behavior

Manipulators are always hard to confront, but covert manipulators are the worst. When confronted, they will remain cool as a cucumber and yet rigid and unbending. When you begin to spot their flawed logic, you might start to get frustrated. If you continue to argue with them, it'll be hard for you not to raise your voice a bit. You'll start to look like the irrational one, and they'll try to take back control based on their "maturity" in remaining calm.

It's tempting to defend yourself and try to get the other person to see what's really going on. But a true manipulator is not going to change their tune, and the more you give in to that temptation to defend yourself, the more they will continue twisting your words. It won't be long before you find yourself trapped in that distorted web of lies and false perceptions. If you're in a situation with a true manipulator, your two goals for any confrontation that occurs should be to diffuse and exit, whether that means exiting the current conversation or exiting the friendship. Avoid insults, arguments, losing your temper, accusing the other person of manipulation, or getting overly emotional. When you speak, stick to statements that are truthful, objective, and peaceful.

There are aspects of dealing with a manipulative person who requires high maturity, patience, or self-discipline. You may not have the self-control to respond without losing your temper and making the situation worse. If that is the case, accept this about yourself and take extra steps to avoid a nasty confrontation (for example, invite a mediator into the discussion or send an email rather than talk in person, so you have time to think through what you are saying) (for example, invite a mediator into the discussion or send an email rather than talk in person, so you have time to think through what you are saying).

For me, it can trigger a bit of anxiety to deal with someone who loses his temper. In order to feel secure in scenarios that had a lot of potential for blow-ups, I had to bring a friend with me. I realized I wasn't quite in a position to do so as much as I wished I could tackle the conflict on my own. If I had failed to acknowledge this about myself because of my decision to behave harsher than I was, I would have endured a lot of needless anxiety. Don't wish you were better than you are at coping with the situation. There will be individuals undermining the vulnerable points and trying to make it seem like it should be easier for you to manage the situation than it is. Don't equate your reaction to someone else's response to a situation.

Ignoring What They Do And Say

Manipulative individuals are supposed to be neglected. When you try to keep them accountable, these people flip flop on problems, are slippery, promise to support that never comes, and continuously make you feel bad—all you don't want in person. The biggest mistake you can make when dealing with a dishonest person is trying to correct them. You fall deeper into their pit by correcting them. Manipulative individuals can use frustration and uncertainty to bait you into a confrontation. In order to see how you tick, they want to make you emotional. They'll use them to manipulate your decisions until they know the things that cause you. A smarter approach is to totally disregard them. Just delete them from your life. If you can't immediately erase them, like if they're a boss, coworker, or family member, agree with what they're doing and then go do your own thing anyway.

Hit Their Centre Of Gravity

Manipulative individuals use their own tactics against you constantly. They're going to become friends with your friends, turning them against you. They'll dangle some small prize in front of you and make you chase it endlessly—any time you get close to it, they'll take it away. They'll forever keep past acts over your head. On and on as well. Avoid letting people who are manipulative use their tactics against you. Turn the tables instead. Build your own plan and hit them where it hurts. If you are forced to deal with a manipulative person who tries to make your life hell, no matter how hard you try to ignore them, you have only one choice, finding and attacking their center of gravity. This center may be the associates, followers, or subordinates of the deceptive person. It may be a high-level talent or a sophisticated knowledge of a specific area. It may be a specific resource they control.

Either way, figure out what their center of gravity is and make it yours. Build allies with individuals close to them, recruit individuals to replace them with their skillsets and knowledge base, or siphon away their valuable resources. This will throw them off balance and cause them, not yours, to concentrate on managing their lives.

Trust Your Judgment

You know better than anyone else what's best for your life. So many individuals go around asking for the advice of other people on everything. What am I supposed to make of my life? What good am I at? And who am I? To describe you, stop searching for other individuals. Defining yourself. Trust in yourself. What distinguishes winners from losers is not the ability to listen to other people's beliefs; it is the ability to listen to the beliefs of one's own. You prevent deceptive people from influencing your life by forming your own values and holding on to them firmly. Your convictions will serve as a blockade in this manner, keeping manipulators ostracized and out of your way.

Don't pretend to blend in

Try to reinvent yourself. A misconception is a notion that continuity is somehow virtuous or tied to achievement. Manipulative people want you to be consistent in order to drive their agendas forward, so they can count on you. Every day at 9 am, they want you to wake up and work for them for the minimum wage. They want you to come home and clean the house on time to make them feel good about themselves.

Lines of assembly are consistent. The prison will be constant. Consistency is how you are maintained in a box by manipulators. It's how you are dominated by them. The only way to stop being exploited is by constantly going against all the constraints that others are trying to set for you.

Avoid trying to fit yourself in. Work to stand out instead. Act in every possible way to be different and never remain the same for too long. Personal growth requires a lack of continuity, by definition. Constant change—constant reinvention—is necessary.

Stop Compromising

Guilt is an emotion that is pointless. But it's a good weapon. Guilt is one of the weapons that can be used against you by manipulative individuals. They're going to make you feel bad for past defeats and minor mistakes, or they're going to make you feel guilty for being overconfident and prideful. They'll use it against you every time you spend feeling satisfied or sure of yourself. No one should ever feel too good; they'll say about themselves.

Another tool that can be used by manipulators against you is doubt. They will work to instill within you a sense of self-doubt—doubt about your skills and you're worth. Their general aim is to throw you off balance and make you guess yourself second. In this state of incertitude, manipulators gain control. They are twice as likely to persuade you to compromise on your beliefs, your goals, and yourself, and their impact becomes greater.

The answer is easy—avoid feeling guilty. Avoid self-doubting. You do not owe anyone anything when it comes to your own life. You deserve to make yourself feel comfortable and to be proud of your achievements. You deserve to have a good sense of trust and self-confidence in what you do. Compromising on all of these topics is not moral or enlightened. It's the road to self-destruction instead.

Never ask for permission

Forgiveness is easier to ask for than permission. The issue is that we've been taught to ask for permission constantly. We had to beg for everything we wanted as a child-to-be fed, altered, and burped. We had to ask permission to go to the bathroom during school, and we had to wait for lunch at a set time and wait for our turn to play with toys. As a consequence, most individuals never stop waiting for permission.

Employees worldwide are waiting to be promoted and waiting for their chance to talk. Most are so used to being selected that they sit in meetings quietly, fearful of speaking out of turn or even raising their hands. There is another way to live.

What if whenever you wanted to do it, you did whatever you wanted to do? What if you avoided being too concerned and made people feel secure with politeness? What if you live your life exactly the way you want to, instead? These are all things at any time that you can do.

Manipulative individuals want you to feel beholden to some imaginary law or ideal that says that you cannot take action freely without consulting either an authoritative figure or some party. The reality is at any moment, and you can ignore this sense of confinement. Today, you will begin living your life drastically different from the life you lived yesterday. It is yours to make the decision.

Develop a greater sense of purpose

Destiny-driven people are not easily fooled. In this country, the reason manipulators continue to flourish is that so many people live purposeless lives. You'll believe something when your life lacks meaning. Nothing you'll do. And nothing matters, actually.

Individuals that lack motive are just wasting time. No rhyme or reason is behind how they live their lives. They have no idea where they are going or why they are here. So, they work in meaningless jobs and stuff their heads full of celebrity news, reality TV, and other kinds of useless knowledge to keep from going mad. They keep busy to stop the feeling of hopeless loneliness from rising inside of them. This profession and emptiness empower individuals who are deceptive.

Every minute, a sucker is born there. You're the sucker if you're constantly distracted, constantly consuming pointless information, continually trying to keep busy. By peddling meaningless knowledge and behaviors to them, manipulators monitor purposeless individuals. Developing a sense of destiny is the only way to avoid this fate. Fate kills diversion. Manipulators can't hurt you when you know you're going. You can't be disturbed or misguided by them.

Keep Taking New Opportunities

In one basket, the universe needs you to position your eggs. You are advised to lock yourself into a lease, a car payment, a stable relationship, a single office work, on and on, by everyone and all around you. They want you to stay for the rest of your life, stacked down to a single chance.

Being optimistic is also looked down on nowadays. It is also seen that hunger is a sign of weakness. Why can't you satisfy yourself with what you've got? Why would you be so greedy? When you show a desire for more, this is what manipulative individuals would ask you. They're going to call you greedy, arrogant, prideful. They're going to make you feel cold and uncomfortable like you're heartless and inhumane. The truth of the matter is that they want to keep you in your place. They want you to remain in the same job and live for the rest of your life in the same place. They want you to remain

DARK PSYCHOLOGY SECRETS AND MANIPULATION

dependent on them and the processes they govern. The only way to remain independent is to actively search out new opportunities and build them. Continue to apply for new jobs, start new companies, continue developing new relationships, and keep seeking new experiences.

Stop being a child

Suppose you're fooled once by another; shame on them. If you get fooled ten times by others, you're an idiot. Avoid having manipulators all over you to walk. Avoid being a bag for punching. Nobody feels bad for you, and you just embarrass yourself. Have enough self-consciousness and self-respect to say no to people who are dishonest.

You can't just walk around life blaming the concerns on other people. You can't just stroll through life unaware of individuals trying to deceive you, either. Yeah, there are negative and deceptive individuals. And yes, these people will try to use you. That doesn't say, though, that you get a free pass to make errors and be used.

Without your consent, no one can control you. You're accountable for your own wins and shortcomings. If you are out-strategized by others—it is your responsibility, not theirs. Be responsible. Learn from your mistakes. Don't continue to trust the same slippery person over and over again. Slice them loose. Remove your life from them. Limit yourself to being surrounded by like-minded people who are not going to use you.

Betting on yourself

Take a gamble on the one thing in life that you can control—yourself. Too many individuals limit themselves to considering only external factors when it comes to making difficult decisions. The financial and relationship implications of a situation are considered by them. Yet, they fail to acknowledge the impact on their personal satisfaction and sense of self-worth that their choice would have. As a consequence, while they should be taking risks on themselves, they take chances on other individuals. So they wonder why they are wretched.

You put yourself at the hands of those people and stuff when you just take chances on external individuals and things. This makes you vulnerable to coercion and juicy. Instead, you should take your own chances. Don't ask questions like, "Who is the better person to side with in any difficult situation you're facing?" or "Which is more likely to be a successful option?" "Ask instead, What do I want the most to do? 'And then go and do it out.

For example, if you're faced with a chance to start your own company or stay at the same dead-end job, don't just stay at the job because the pay is just slightly pathetic. Don't only stay when there are just marginally unhappy relationships. You're betting on external factors when you do this. This is always an error. Betting on yourself is a safer approach.

You will never regret making bets on yourself. Of course, you will have to take full responsibility for any errors you make. Sure, you're going to have to keep yourself at a higher level. Yet you will be entirely accountable for your own victories as well. You will keep rising and reaching higher and higher levels of performance.

Avoid Emotional Attachment With Them

Anything you do is wrong with a manipulator. Any battle you've had is the fault of you. Being tampered with will wreak havoc on your feelings. You go from crying to being furious to, in short order, feeling bad and worthless. You're sorry, then that you didn't stand up for yourself. You're ashamed of letting them get over you again. Your feelings are more stable when you leave a manipulator. Life is a journey that is adventurous. Along the way, at various times, many people come to give us company for a certain period of time and go after playing their role in our lives. The coming and going of the people in themselves is no problem, but the problems occur when you become emotionally attached to the people and feel powerless, tense, and worried when the relationship ends with an emotional manipulator in particular. Therefore, if you want to stay satisfied and make strides in life, then as early as possible, you need to resolve emotional attachment.

There is no question that the driving force for you to step down in the chosen direction is certain individuals. But when you're away from them, you should be careful not to get distracted. You need to make judicious use of relationships. Be linked and take care of individuals with a disconnected approach to build a trustworthy environment. However, when you let them go out of your life because you are a manipulator, you should not be dependent on those people for your growth and stop your life because some other relationship is waiting on your path to your journey. Leaving behind the memories of the past, you need to re-focus on your path.

Emotional attachment handling measures the level of maturity and seriousness of your journey to the chosen route. The moment you spend with people enjoys it. Learn from them, love them, and take care of them, but do not make sticks for them to walk. Most of the time, people normally fear losing someone because of their inability to step on in life alone. So you don't need to resolve emotional attachment anymore if you dare to walk alone on the chosen path.

Meditate Regularly

Are you interested in getting a calmer feeling? More focused? More power over your feelings? If so, in today's fast-paced, high-tech, busy world, meditation can offer mental stability, which many people long for. Meditation will help provide the relaxation and clarity you search for in just a few minutes a day if you deal with depression, mood swings, stress, or other related problems.

Everyone will benefit from frequent meditation, whether the challenges you face are due to depression and stress, past trauma, or a chemical shift in brain function. Really there is no better time than today to start meditating! Over time, the effects of meditation build-up, but you can almost instantly feel a sense of relaxation, quiet, and peace.

Meditation takes the body into a deep relaxation state and offers the required tools and support to cope with stress. The mind calms, and the body enters a state of tranquility as the body and mind learn to relax by deep breathing exercises and techniques.

The harmful effects of stress hormones that overtax your body and your emotional state can potentially be neutralized by meditation. Emotions relax and regulate as hormone concentrations return to normal. And you'll be better able to cope with strong feelings and circumstances the next time you feel frustrated or nervous, using your breath to calm down and relax. Emotions can really keep you hostage, making you feel like you're living your life on a roller coaster with ups and downs, twists and turns that are uncontrollable. On the other hand, meditation requires a lot of imagination, a powerful technique that can help you reshape your present way of thinking and create a more positive, healthy emotional environment.

Meditation will assist you in the present moment to develop self-esteem, recover from past traumas, and feel more joy. Visualization not only provides you with the resources to cope with emotional anger by providing stability during meditation, but it can also help you plan out a path of transformation for your future. From the inside out, meditation will change your life and help you cope with emotional manipulators.

Inspire Them

To help them become their best selves, use all the experience you have learned about being your best self, too. When you're having trouble modifying their actions, work with a counselor. It can be very difficult to alter their actions, and you may not be able to do it on your own. A therapist or psychologist may assist him in recognizing habits that need to alter and discuss their feelings. They're also going to help him learn new practices that are safer for him.

Say "You're right" to them

This begins with no longer reacting the way you used to their techniques. If you don't want to, you say "no or speak your mind, even if they don't like it. Work on feeling okay about how they will respond negatively. Don't pick it up if it isn't yours. Your actions can only be monitored. That's crucial because you're not going to be able to alter a manipulator's actions, but you can avoid being their victim. That happens when you begin to say "no." We are exploited because we accept it, and the first step in breaking the cycle is to refuse to be manipulated. Manipulators are successful at what they do, so pay attention to the response they get. Things that tug on the heartstrings are likely to be said or done. In our "no," we should stand firm, recognizing that we are taking the first step to liberate ourselves from their power.

Let Go Of Unhealthy Relationships

Toxic interactions can be tough to let go of. In a loop of going back to relationships that are not good for them, several individuals get trapped. This just produces a spiral of hurt and sorrow. There are ways to let go of relationships that are toxic. Psychologists have consulted enough with individuals who have had this issue to be able to write a complete handbook on the subject.

To free yourself from a toxic relationship, the very first step is to admit to yourself that the relationship is not okay. The symptoms of a toxic relationship can be found, and try to explain them to yourself. It's called cognitive dissonance' if you experience the awkward feeling in the back of your mind, and it's your brain trying to shield you from what you know is real. Take note of the things that make you feel this way in a relationship. The first step is recognizing that your relationship is toxic. You have to be mindful of all the things that are affecting you before you can truly be free.

A two-way street is partnerships. Two parties are involved in the relationship, which means that two people are interested in all the disputes, conflicts, and actions. You can't take yourself solely to blame. If you blame yourself for all the relationship issues, you're going to find yourself going back and trying to resolve them. Recognize that both sides are often to blame for a dysfunctional relationship. Recognize your tasks, but only your obligations. In a toxic relationship, you don't need to put up with someone else's issues. There is no need to hoist it on yourself because you're not to blame.

When trying to let go of a controlling partner, cutting off touch is one of the best things you can do. Holding in touch would just make it harder to let go. This means following up on toxic people who are not in your life anymore. Resist scrolling through their social media or asking how they're doing with their mutual friends. You should always follow your instincts when it comes to cutting individuals out of your life, according to Sarah Newman, M.A. Even though it can sound drastic, Newman recommends loosening the bonds when it comes to a toxic relationship. You need to be in a state where you can feel neutral about the lack of touch rather than pain to move on.

Mariana Bockarova, Ph.D., notes that one of the best ways to move on from a fractured and manipulative relationship is closure. Bockarova agrees that resolution will allow people in a safe and positive way to rebuild their entire lives. One way to help you let go of a toxic relationship is to find closure. The closing comes from inside for a lot of individuals and remembering all the ways the partnership went wrong in the first place. For others, it may bring closure by writing one more letter or making the other person recognize their toxicity. Whatever it is for moving forward, the resolution is critical

In leaving any dysfunctional relationship and letting it go, the most important thing is getting someone there to catch you if you fall. It can be jarring to let go, particularly if they are long-term. Get together with friends and family who, during more stressful times, will help encourage you. When it comes to not seeking out individuals you have already cut off, they will also help hold you responsible. When it comes to letting go of unhealthy partnerships, support networks are invaluable. Don't fear reaching out to the ones who love you the most.

Build A Strong Mentality

Although one toxic person may use deception and lies, another may resort to threats and incivility. And if you're not careful, you can take a severe toll on your well-being from people like that. However, emotionally intense individuals work in a professional way with deceptive individuals. They refuse to give their control away, and no matter who surrounds them, they continue being their best self.

Putting a name on your emotions reduces their strength. So if you're feeling sad, nervous, frustrated, or afraid, acknowledge it—at least to yourself. Also, pay attention to the way certain emotions can influence your actions. You may be less likely to take chances when you feel nervous. You can be more impulsive when you are excited. Increasing your understanding of your feelings will reduce the risk of making unreasonable choices based on emotions.

Naming your feelings is just part of the fight—you will need skills to handle your feelings. Think of your existing skills for coping. When you're nervous, can you eat? To calm down, do you drink? When you're upset, do you vent to your friends? When you're worried, should you stay at home? These popular techniques may make you feel better at the moment, but over the long term, they will make you feel worse.

Look for coping skills that, over the long-term, are good for you. Bear in mind that what works for one person will not always work for you, so you need to figure out what is best for you to cope with your feelings. To find out what works for you, experiment with different coping abilities; deep breathing, exercising, meditating, reading, painting, and spending time in nature are only a few of the techniques that might help.

How you feel and how you act influences the way you think. It robs you of mental strength by saying things like, "I can't stand this or "I'm such an idiot," Pay heed to your feelings. Popular themes and trends you'll probably find. You might be talking yourself out of doing stuff that feels scary. Or maybe you are persuaded that you don't have power over your life.

React with something more constructive to unproductive and unreasonable thinking. But instead of thinking, "I'm going to mess this up," tell yourself, "This is my chance to shine, and I'm going to do my best." The most instrumental thing you can do to change your life can be to change your conversations with yourself.

By modifying your actions, the best way to train your brain to think differently is to Do hard things—and keep doing them even though you think you can't. You are going to prove to yourself that you are better than you believe. Also, develop good daily habits. Practice kindness, work out, get plenty of sleep, and eat a balanced diet so that the brain and body can be at their best. Look for individuals who inspire you to be your best. And build an atmosphere that supports your efforts to develop a healthier lifestyle.

If you do them right alongside your unhealthy habits, all the good habits in the world won't be effective. It's like eating donuts on a treadmill when you're racing. Pay attention to your bad habits that drain mental power from you (we all have them). It just takes one or two to keep you stuck in life, whether you feel sorry for yourself or you envy the success of other people. When you become conscious of your bad habits, devote resources to replacing them with healthy choices. You will then be able to step out of the hamster wheel and move forward towards your goals, in fact.

Much as it takes time and practice to become physically strong, it also takes determination to develop mental strength. But the secret to feeling your best and achieving your full potential is to develop mental muscles.

Giving yourself positive self-talk all day long

Your attitude will totally tarnish an emotional manipulator, so make sure you restore yourself during the day with uplifting self-talks.—of us has a series of messages that are playing in our minds over and over. This internal debate or personal commentary deceives our responses to life and its situations. One way optimism, hope, and joy can be appreciated, encouraged, and maintained are to consciously fill our minds with optimistic self-talk.

Too often, because of our manipulative spouse, the pattern of self-talk we've formed is negative. We recall the negative things our partners, parents, siblings, or teachers told us as children. We recall other kids' negative responses that diminished how we felt about ourselves. These messages have played over and over in our minds over the years, fueling our feelings of anger, fear, remorse, and hopelessness.

Identifying the root of these messages and then working with the client to consciously "overwrite" them is one of the most important avenues used in recovery for those suffering from depression. If a person learned that he was useless as a child, we show him how genuinely unique he is. If a person learned to predict disasters and destructive incidents when growing up, we offer her a better way to foresee the future.

Try the exercise that follows. Write down some of your mind's detrimental signals that undermine your ability to resolve your situation. Be descriptive, wherever possible, and include anyone who contributed to the message that you remember. Now, take a moment to consciously counteract the negative messages in your life with positive truths. If you don't find them fast, don't give up. There is a hopeful truth to any negative message that can override the weight of depression. There are always these truths; keep looking till you find them.

You can have a negative message which replays in your mind anytime you make a mistake. "You have been told as a child, "You can never amount to something or "You can't do anything right." When you make a mistake—and you will because we all do—you can choose to overwrite that message with a positive message, such as "I choose to embrace and grow out of my mistake" or "I become a better person as I learn from my mistakes.

Positive self-talk is not the manipulation of oneself. For eyes that see just what you want to see, it is not mentally looking at situations. Instead, constructive self-talk is about knowing the facts, in the circumstances, and in yourself. The fact that you can make mistakes is one of the universal truths. It is impossible to expect perfection from yourself or someone else. It is also impossible to expect no difficulties in life, whether by your own actions or sheer circumstances.

Positive self-talk tries to pull the positive out of the negative when negative incidents or errors arise, to make you do better, move faster, or just keep going forward. The practice of positive self-talk is also the mechanism that helps you discover the obscured optimism, hope, and joy in any given situation.

CHAPTER ELEVEN:

THE ART OF PEOPLE READING

Where many people go wrong is believing that the message is told by our words alone. In fact, studies show that most communication is not only through words. This is a total misconception. Rather, over 80 percent of the job is done by our tone of voice, emotional expression, and body language, and our words do the rest of it. The key to reading people is to master all of these non-verbal cues, and we will dive into each of them.

Step 2 of mind control and manipulation is where the art of reading people comes in. We dealt with Step 1 in the previous chapter.

Step 1 is all about having proper control of the state and sharpness of perception. We need to have solid-state control when we want to get into the mind of the subject so we don't lose control of the situation, which will undoubtedly happen if we let the subject be the one that influences us.

Perceptual sharpness enters the image mostly for the collection of information. You can't expect to, after all, enter the mind of a person you barely know. In order to use those dark psychological techniques on them, you have to know them incredibly well. Obviously, perceptual sharpness is a massive part of people's reading. You will not be able to read these indications if you don't even enter the communication signals that the subject gives you. Long story short: perceptual sharpness and state control are both necessary to use any of the techniques in this book. Step 2 is what comes after the learning of these two necessary skills. We're going to spend some time discussing the idea behind this move and what happens in Step 3 after it. Then we're going to spend the rest of the chapter going through the various unconscious signs that people use to interact to tell you what they say.

We use the perceptual sharpness and state regulation we have planned for in Step 1 to achieve one goal and one goal alone when we get into Step 2: mimic their unconscious contact signals. Now there's a lot in that sentence to break down, so let's get started. We are not talking about something invisible when we suggest the subject shows unconscious signs of contact. We are talking about evident habits—anyone can see them, but you can easily overlook them without sufficiently strong perceptual sharpness.

What are those kinds of behaviors? They are the various behaviors of body language; the different concepts we convey in different ways by using our voices, the messages we deliver through different eye contact levels, and finally, the messages we relay through the facial expressions we give other people.

The second part of this chapter deals with the basic meanings behind all these distinct signs of contact. Collecting this data is immensely helpful in monitoring or manipulating them efficiently, but that is not what this first section is about.

Second, in mind control and conditioning, we are focused on these unconscious communication signals as they apply to Phase 2. And we have already outlined how they apply to it. You have to mimic the signs that your subject is showing. In Step 2, this is what you've got to do.

It is straightforward but efficient. By doing this, you do much of what you have to do to get into the mind of the subject. So you know why you need to know more about how the brain works, especially how the subconscious works. One of the exciting topics that we research in Dark Psychology is the unconscious mind. We all have a knowledge of what the unconscious mind is, but to put it in plain English: all the things we know are in the unconscious mind but are not sure of understanding. Without really going into the deep territory, we can think of examples of stuff like this. Find the things with your hands that you perform. You have actively stopped worrying about how to move your body to swing on a playground or how to ride a bicycle. You learned these skills so long ago that your unconscious mind is actually part of your procedural memory. At this point, it would be hard for you to even try to think about this stuff when you were doing them.

Your mind is still unconscious. The big thing to remember is that this doesn't mean you are still unconscious in these areas of your mind. It's just that when we need to, we just make them aware, and sometimes when we use them, we don't really need to make them conscious, just as when we ride a bike. We may use this implicit procedural memory without consciously thinking about it.

We're talking about the unconscious mind because the way our minds communicate with the outside world is our unconscious sign of communication. People don't knowingly use these body language instruments, eye contact, and so on. Without even thinking about it, we all do them. This suggests that the unconscious signs of communication are like the window into our unconscious mind that we offer people. Without even understanding it, we expose our minds to individuals. In the next part, where we tell you what the most important signs mean, this is what we will get to.

But we want to do more than interpret individual signals in phase 2. We want to break into their unconsciousness deep down. That's why we copy their signals. The amount of eye contact we make is close. We hold our hands the same way, do similar things with our voices, and when necessary, match the emotion the subject expresses. In Step 2, we do this because this helps the subject integrate us into their unconscious mind. After this is done, Phase 3 is simply to get the data from their heads, substitute it with fresh concepts, or give them the idea of following a new action, all while pretending that this is their definition.

New students of dark psychology prefer to fear that the subject will realize that they mimic them. But our lesson on solipsism, you've got to remember. If they see you imitating them, they'll just think you're doing it yourself unconsciously, even if that's not your aim. In their unconsciousness, you want to put them entirely at ease, so much so that you become part of their minds without even realizing it. It goes much deeper than we said it would. Since most of the human mind is unconscious, that implies that the mind's language is unconscious. Unconscious communication signals such as eye contact, emotion, body language, and tone of voice are all ways that the outside world shows itself to our unconscious minds. This mode of communication's less-than-obvious existence shows the nature of the mind's language.

The language spoken by our brains is very distinct from the language in which this book is written or any language other than English. It has three key features that we will discuss quickly: (1) the mind's language is about instincts, (2) it's nonverbal, and (3) it's developing. Let's delve into what they mean in more detail now that you know all of these functions. If we say the language of the unconscious human mind is instinctual, we suggest that things like people appear to do are not "overthink." This also indicates that the unconscious mind has no potential to deceive. The mind can't filter it no matter how impolite or crass the message that it sends might be. It's going to convey the message exactly as it is, and it doesn't know how else to do it.

To understand this, you should think back to the example of riding your bike. From reading a textbook, you do not understand how to do it. It took time and maturity for the ability to be mastered. It was all instinct after that. You may have some ideas about what to say if someone specifically asked you how it was done, but it wouldn't be enough to get that person to learn. Much the same way you did, they'd have to do it. It has to become instinct because their unconscious mind is where they know how to do things like riding bikes; it cannot be mastered by reading words.

The next characteristic of the brain's language is that it is nonverbal. Our minds do not use words the way we do, as we said before. Of course, we can read and write sentences because our brains can understand a language like English. But the point here is that when we are talking about the language of the brain, this is just the tip of the iceberg.

In a way that goes beyond words, the brain is capable of interpreting the universe. Another way to put it is that you can understand stuff without having the words for it because you are your brain at the end of the day. Many of us in our day-to-day lives witness this. We also have thoughts and opinions about the world we live in, but that doesn't mean that we have essays about every topic ready to go if we are asked about it. Just for the sake of proving this, answer this question in your mind very quickly: What do you think about the issue of global waste?

When we asked, you had thoughts about this right away. When you are specifically asked a question, your brain has no choice but to come up with some form of an answer, and this is another thing that you can take advantage of when you manipulate someone's mind. However, it doesn't say that you've got a completely thought-out, eloquent answer ready to go. You would have an eloquent reaction to this if you happened to have done a lot of research about it before. But even so, with every single central question we might ask you, you will still not have a complete paragraph ready to go.

This is the best way of understanding the nonverbal existence of the language of the brain. Without using words, the brain is capable of thinking about things. That's why, through all the channels we discussed, your brain communicates itself unconsciously: eye contact, body language, speech, and emotion.

Of course, the limits of our unconscious minds are not limited to these cold signs of contact. They are only one manner in which it expresses itself. The best thing you can do for yourself to progress in dark psychology might be to get to understand the ramifications of the fact that your brain thinks nonverbally. The minds of other people are nonverbal, much like yours. Once you understand how to talk nonverbally with your own brain, you can do the same to gain mind control and manipulation with someone else. The last primary aspect of the mind's language is that it is continually changing. We'll have to step back and analyze the make-up of the brain to explain this.

The scientific name for the cells of your brain is 'Neuron.' Your neurons, on their own, do nothing valuable in your brain. The importance of your neurons lies in the relationships they form with each other. These links go beyond just sending each other messages: you keep repeating the key ideas again and again as you learn something. Repetition is an important part of learning because before the connection eventually becomes really powerful, you have to continue strengthening the same relationships between your neurons. The term for this is the law of Hebb: the more times those neurons make links with each other, the more they "wire" together into a long-lasting bond. The reverse is also true: if a connection between neurons is not improved for a long time, the wiring will become weaker before another connection inevitably makes way.

There is only so much space in your brain for connections, so making new connections and losing old ways are both important aspects of the memory process. The language of the brain is made entirely of memory at the end of the day, and everything in your brain is some form of memory. In English or any other language, these memories are not "written" because they are nonverbal. Since our longest-lasting memories are the ones with the most emotionally resonant content, they are incredibly close to gut feelings.

The term "firing" is used to make new connections or reinforce existing connections. This is called "pruning" when you neglect connections between your neurons. You should also know that synapses are the scientific term for the links between your neurons. We will simply name them connections or synaptic connections in this book.

When you imitate the external expression of the language of the subject, which comes in the form of body language, speech, eye contact, and emotion, bear in mind all three characteristics of the language of the mind. If you are experienced in perceptual sharpness, learning from these signals can come to you more quickly. When you get good at putting all these pieces together, by being fully in tune with their brain's language, you will be able to put the topic at ease.

Since all of this is unconscious, they're not even going to be able to suggest that you should get this way into their brain. Yet, it is something incredibly satisfying to do. Just one step remains from there: Step 3. Phase 3 is where you fill in whatever tool you use to obtain mind control or coercion. A lot of learners of dark psychology go wrong by assuming they should skip to Phase 3 directly. Also, after the subject completely engages them in reciprocating their feelings, they believe the subject will listen to everything they say, even though they do not show state power. Even after barely understanding anything about the topic, they believe the matter would listen to them because they have not honed their perceptual sharpness.

These, of course, just cover Stage 1. Step 2 is where things get even more complicated. Although it is possible to unravel the mysterious language of the brain when you devote yourself to it, this task is far from an easy one to finish. Not only do you have to understand the brain language's three key characteristics, but you have to devote yourself to understanding all the numerous messages that our subjects will give us with their body language. There is no point in jumping straight to step 3 if you don't do steps 1 and 2 first, as many beginners do. Thankfully, you're not going to make this mistake because you've come so far already, and the last thing you need to finish is learning Step 2 to get through the end of this chapter.

All we have left for Phase 2, the art of reading people, is to learn the different basic messages transmitted by all the unconscious contact signals that we have addressed. We're going to get straight to it without further ado.

Dark Psychology And Body Language

Perhaps the first thing we note about them might be the amount of eye contact the subject makes with us. Whether or not the judgments we make of them are correct based on this, it is nonetheless valid that we assess them for it. It seems that the amount of eye contact with us speaks volumes. When someone has a lot of eye contact with you and what it really means when they don't, you need to know what it really means.

In the popular imagination, it is a common misconception that individuals who do not make eye contact signal that they are "submissive" to you. This is flat-out false, and if you believe that you will only be vulnerable to being taken advantage of by others, stick with this assumption.

Two things depend on the amount of eye contact someone makes, and only two things: personality and social background.

It is easier to describe the first one. Naturally, certain individuals make more eye contact, and if this has to do with biology or the environment in which they were raised, there is only one thing about this. Since this is who they are or because of their perceived relationship with you, you have to determine whether the subject has abundant or no eye contact. Only from there can you derive some helpful knowledge from this form of the unconscious speech of your brain.

The social meaning element is a little trickier because it is linked to all the other stuff we use dark psychology for. Nearly all individuals, after all, have less eye contact with people they don't know. It doesn't say anything about how they feel or the first impression they have of that person. That doesn't mean that too much or too little eye contact shouldn't take messages from you. Indeed, too little can mean that they are anxious around you. Too much may mean that they are still nervous around you; however, by overcompensating and attempting to take charge of the situation, they are only coping with it in a different way. In spite of their best intentions, what really happens when someone makes so much eye contact is that they end up apparently trying too hard to be in control.

We all know someone who, time and again, makes this mistake. It's understandable that they're trying to look like the dominant one, but it totally defeats the intent when you make the fact that you're trying to do this too obvious. And that's what it could look like when someone makes too much eye contact with them. But what about eye contact with you? As for the amount of eye contact you can make, there is no simple response. All has to do with the particular topic with which you are interacting. Although one subject will react to a lot of eye contact really well, the next one may be entirely distracted by it and not want to communicate with you.

The general guideline of Phase 2 still refers to eye contact, however. When it occurs in their body language, you want to mimic the manifestation of the unconscious language in their brain. This is also what you can do if the topic is not making too much eye contact, but just a little bit. It shows them that you, without saying it out loud, are like them.

When they make a lot of eye contact, the same thing happens. You're expected to look them a lot in the eye, so they get the message that the two of you are alike. Know that the human mind is unaware, so they make a similar amount of eye contact; they don't say to themselves, "This person is like me." Their brain thinks this, but because it's all unconscious, they don't understand it.

Follow your instincts, especially with eye contact: listen to whatever your perceptual sharpness says to you. Just go along with it, even if it doesn't feel right to you if you find yourself instinctively having a certain amount of eye contact with others. It may feel awkward simply because it's a different degree of eye contact that you're used to, but you can go along with it when your own unconscious sends you signs because of the knowledge you get from perceptual sharpness. It knows better than you do it intentionally.

Our next lesson in communication's unconscious signals is all about the location of the feet of the subject. It may seem a little over-analytical, but it can tell us a lot about what a person feels like. It is particularly helpful because it says nothing about personality.

When they are communicating with you, we refer to the distance between the subject's feet. Simply put, they're playing it safe if their feet are far apart. They still don't feel ready to become vulnerable to you. They feel relaxed with you if their feet are close together and prepared to be vulnerable.

Our bodies do this instinctively, but you are quickly knocked over when your feet are close together. If they're far apart, it's harder to knock you down. On an unconscious level, we understand this. When you are consciously told this, we know it is true.

But sometimes, our ways of physically feeling safer are all about feeling emotionally and socially safe. It's not as if the topic is concerned that you're actually moving them over. They just prepare for whatever the ramifications of their social contact with you are. This gap is the most important thing for you to pay attention to in all their body language because the closer their feet are together, the closer you are to starting with Step 3.

However, that doesn't mean it's the only thing that you can pay attention to. The others are slightly more intuitive, at least. For one, when they feel in control, individuals take up more space. Don't take this to mean that because you certainly can, you have no chance of manipulating or mind-controlling this person. Actually, we can also use the fact that someone feels comfortable for our benefit. It implies that they have their defenses down, and they can be mind readers more quickly. As always, it's just as important to read the individual situation as to read body language.

But it is not enough to pay attention to the individual actions in the subject's body language to understand the signals their unconscious mind is sending us. Another thing for you to pay attention to is any changes you note in their body language, major or minor.

We can tell intuitively, particularly when someone's behavior unexpectedly changes, that a spark in them has gone off. If this spark is good or bad for us, we can even guess. Listen to and follow the impulses that your own unconscious mind tells you.

If anyone behaves oddly, there is no reason for you to be inconspicuous. You don't have to pay attention to the fact that you have detected a shift in the language of your body, but simply ask them, "Are you doing okay?" "It should have been enough. People are always too proud to admit outwardly that they want help, but their unconscious mind continues to send signs that they wish to help to let others know.

This applies specifically to circumstances that include the subject's mental health, but it is not the only application. But when someone's mental wellbeing is on the line, it is important to identify the signs early. This is simply a measure of protection.

Body language is not the only thing that can make you notice: if you happen to know that in their personal lives, the subject is having a hard time, but they seem to be acting even slightly cheerier than they would naturally, there is a good chance that they were overcompensating for how awful on the inside they feel. You should straightforwardly ask them if they need any help or if they want to chat. It will still make them more comfortable around you, even if they don't open up to you that you cared enough to notice and ask.

You should also pay attention to how slowly or rapidly the subject uses their body when watching for specific motions in body language and changes in body language. We're not just talking about the parts of their bodies that you can see; either if they're talking any faster or slower than they normally do, you should also listen.

This is another instance where what matters is the transition of the unconscious signs. For instance, some people just talk faster or slower than others. If they continue to speak this way, it doesn't mean anything, but it could be a sign of something if they change.

Of course, if a person speaks quickly when they wouldn't usually, this is a pretty clear signal that something is nervous about them. This might even mean that they are lying to you.

But all you know is the typical speech rate of people you already know. Fortunately, from the speed of their body language, we can also learn about individuals we don't recognize. For the most part, based on the rate of their body language, you can classify individuals into two groups of personalities. To start with, we're going to tell you how they're divided based on speed. Simply put, people who move their bodies faster and speak faster are sorted into the personality category of Type A, whereas Type B personalities are people who take it slow and talk more slowly. The definitions of these two classes are pretty clear. Form A individuals are more intense, goal-oriented, and neurotic. Type B individuals, meanwhile, are less anxious and more concentrated on the moment.

There is no particular value judgment you can make between these two classes; both are simply distinct groups of individuals that look differently at life. You should also bear in mind that people in any situation are divided equally and specifically into these two classes. This is because of social forces' influence. You may find yourself around your family as more of Type A and around your friends as more of Type B, or vice versa.

That said, while the definitions aren't accurate, that doesn't mean they're not helpful. You can use the strategies you learn from dark psychology on them differently until you have an understanding of who individuals are based on the speed of their actions. As we often say, you cannot use these strategies on all persons in the same way, so it is incredibly useful to be able to make different decisions depending on whether they are Type A or B.

Voice and emotions are two fields that are different from body language in nonverbal communication, but they are both highly significant. The way somebody's voice is used shows you a lot about them. We seem to think that people are just born with their voice, and that is the end of that. It is partly true, of course, that we must use the voice we are given. But the problem with this deception of mind is that no matter what kind of voice we are naturally provided, we can do a lot with our voices. Take your voice's pitch as an example. To some extent, as we said, this isn't something we can manage. Many of us have a particular pitch range that our voice naturally chooses to go to. However, we also know that if we so choose, we can have a lot of control over where we take our voices within this context.

Your voice's pitch tells the person you're talking to a few things about you. For one, research indicates that individuals are more attentive to higher-pitched voices. This makes a lot of sense, mainly because it's easier to hear higher-pitched voices than lower pitches. In the sound of monotone, lower pitches can go too far in a way that prevents us from understanding the speaker.

However, this isn't the only side of the story. From the same studies, we also know that individuals appear to take lower-pitched voices more seriously. In another book, some of the social problems behind this fact may be explored, but the reality is, this can be generalized to both men and women. When they want to sound more serious, both sexes prefer to try to lower their voices.

Our propensity to do this has contributed to the condition now known as vocal fry. Vocal fry is the word for when people go too low in pitch for the natural range of their voice, just too little bit too far. It makes us sound gravelly and unnatural when we do that. You have to balance it to make sure it doesn't sound fake, even knowing that people could take you more seriously with a lower voice.

Now when paying attention to our subjects, there are a lot of things we can take away from this study. For one thing, if we hear in their voice a vocal fry, that means they're putting us on a front. They want us to be more serious about them. To our benefit, we can use this knowledge to try to get something from them in return for letting them know that we take them seriously.

As with nonverbal communication, the second significant part of our voices segues nicely into the last area of unconscious communication signals: emotion. In our accents, as well as in our facial expressions, we communicate feelings. We picked up things from the people around us, so as always, we should just listen to our perceptual sharpness to figure out what these feelings should mean.

We instructed you to mimic the unconscious signs of the subject, but this does not always mean doing exactly as they do. A great demonstration of this is the case of emotion. If the subject shows that they are angry about something in their voice and face, that doesn't mean you can exactly match their emotions.

You should definitely express emotions in a way that affirms your feelings. Don't get us wrong. You never want to make the subject think that you don't take their feelings seriously, and to do that often requires emotions we don't feel natural to take on. For this reason, state control is a required skill. But you don't just get as angry as they get. They are, after all, the only one who is allowed to be as mad as they are, the one who has experienced whatever trigger they have experienced. If you acted as upset about it as they did, it would appear unnatural.

Express a similar emotion instead, but at a slightly lower intensity. If the individual is totally furious, they just seem mad. If they look angry, they seem annoyed, and so on. By mirroring them back to the subject, you want to affirm their emotions, but don't take it too far. Even though this chapter focuses on Step 2 of mind control and the meaning of all the unconscious communication signals, since it is highly intertwined with emotional expression, there is a technique we want to run through. This is the memory activation technique.

Memory activation is a technique that can be used to manipulate behavior for any mind control. While you have a casual conversation with the subject, you get them to talk about a positive memory that is very important to them. The general principle behind it is nothing hard to get your head around. You don't want them to know that this is what you are doing on purpose. You have to make it a priority that they see this as naturally coming up, whatever you do to get this memory to come up. But to bring up the emotional content it has, you want them to remember this experience. The real memory itself, for the purposes of dark psychology, does not matter to you. The only thing you care about is allowing them to once again experience the good feelings associated with the memory.

You will recall how the brain at the microscopic level is structured. The trillions of synaptic links between our neurons are composed of our memories. We're not just storing new memories there, as if we were capturing a video. In order to save space and allow us to remember more things, we constantly make new connections and create associations between things.

This means that the subject not only relates the recollection of the positive emotion and feels it again, but when they experienced this positive emotion, you were around the subject, they will now associate the positive emotion with you. It helps them think of us more positively when we get people to experience good feelings about us. This makes it easier to influence and manipulate their minds.

When it comes to an understanding of the messages that people send us, this is all. They are the portals into the minds of their unconscious, allowing us both to read and control them. You will learn how to lie effectively in the next chapter, which is a crucial skill to have as a Dark Psychology learner. It is a complete analysis of all of its own, but the lessons you have learned so far can still be brought in to succeed in it.

Let's start off.

CHAPTER TWELVE:

HOW TO DECEIVE OTHERS AROUND YOU

O ut there, you can find a lot of books on how to know when someone is lying, but it's very taboo to say how you can be a good liar yourself. It shouldn't even be taboo because sometimes, all of us have to lie. It is a simple fact of life that we cannot tell the truth all the time. Lies need not be important. The main thoughts behind lying well are the same whether you plan to tell big lies or little ones.

Of course, all of the things we apply to dark psychology involve a certain amount of lying, at least lying in the word's typical definition. That means if you want to mind reading, mind control, or manipulate anybody, you have to become an adept liar yourself. Throughout the book, we alluded to the idea of framing. If you didn't know what it meant beforehand, you must have gotten a good idea of it through context, but now is the time to formally go over these concepts, as they are essential ideas for a good liar to learn.

You're not going to be able to tell just one lie if you have to deceive somebody. If this were the case, it would be a lot easier, but the reality is a lot harder than this. You have to construct an entire reality that must be bought into by the listener or subject. That is what makes it so tough to lie, which is why most individuals do not make good liars. As we all do, they might get away with a few lies, but if they go further than that, all the lies they have to say to back up the first lie will overtake them.

That is why more than one lie needs to be told by a good liar. The consequence of telling one small lie without planning for it is that by justifying the first lie with a lot of other lies, it has to make up for this mistake later. This is not important, however, if you are a student of dark psychology. You should learn framing and adaptability principles so that you can be prepared to construct any set of lies that are necessary for whatever situation you are in. The basic concept behind framing may be understood, but you also need to understand how adaptability works into it. Framing is nothing without adaptability, after all. Your adaptability, depending on how individuals react to it, is your ability to adjust your system. You're not going to know how people respond to your deception, so you have to be prepared, good or bad, for any reaction that they have to it.

If they respond in a suspicious way to your deception, this is about the worst thing that can happen. But it doesn't have to say that you get caught in a lie with strong adaptability. And what makes framing and adaptability such a potent combination lies herein. With these two together, you are not only prepared for any potential change in the social environment, but you could also be explicitly challenged to say less than the reality, and you could still get away with it with ample adaptability.

Deception is not an easy thing to do, and that's why most people are not qualified enough to be successful liars. You can't only make it nice enough for it to be plausible if you want to deception the facts in a certain way. You have to make the subject think you are really telling things as they are. That means you don't get to stretch things too far or be too unrealistic. To some extent, your lies need to fit into the real world that everyone else witnesses.

While your deception needs to adapt, this is not all that adaptability is. Not only does your deception have to adjust, but you have to be able to change your own unconscious cues of communication based on the kinds of people you are lying to. You can refer to other chapters to master this aspect of deceiving people correctly because you won't be able to do it effectively without that knowledge.

When you hear about dark psychology, the number one most valuable thing you can take away from it is the similarity—if not absolutely equal—of everyone's experience as a person. You largely know what it is like to be someone else only by living as a human being yourself. That does not mean you know every experience of their existence, but you still know more than is essential to mind control, exploit, and deceive them.

No matter who you are talking to, when you are in the same real-world setting, you have a lot of things in common. No matter how different you think you are personality-wise, it doesn't matter. You look at the surroundings you both have. They may not see precisely the same thing you see but what they see is almost e exactly the same.

This reality can be crucial in deceiving others when you want to change the world that other people see, but if you are not in contact with the same facts that you are, that can only go so far. Even if you're the world's best liar, you're still just one influence in the life of this topic. You could easily become the greatest influence in the subject's life, but you would still be just one. At some point, you have to learn humility. You have to learn that you alone do not determine every little thought that comes across their mind. Only once you reach this point can you become the best liar you can become because you will accept that you have to work with the other information the subject has. Unlike a solipsist, you won't think of yourself as a whole universe that other people have to pay attention to. You will recognize the other universes around you. You will realize that the subject has access to these different influences, too. You have to become more influential than all of these to become the best liar around.

Remember that it is the one who takes command of the narrative that commands the people who believe that narrative. You might not think a lot about narratives anymore, though. It might be that you don't see them as powerful things already, but in all reality, they are. Narratives shape people's way of looking at the world. They even give our lives meaning, and they make us see the light at the end of the tunnel. If a good deceiver comes to us and gives us a narrative that we are prepared to believe, the way we look at the world will change completely.

The best narrative doesn't change how we look at the world, either. They take our world's current ideas and change them just ever so slightly. They have changed so slightly that they have become our permanent way of looking at life, and we don't even remember that we haven't always seen things this way. In different areas of life, you can probably think of examples like this: contemplate whatever instance you think of and seriously consider how you could do this yourself and be the one creating the narrative. This masterful method of slightly but only slightly altering someone is a commonly used one in politics. This is where our following deception technique, which we will call the appeal of identity, comes in. The most versatile deception you can have as a liar is this. That is because the story will still signal to the subject that you are on their side, no matter how many times you have to change your story.

147

No matter if because of adaptation, your story ends up not having to favor the subject, if it still shows them that you are on their side, this is all that matters. Who, for this reason, will always remain with you no matter what. People are kin-centric. As much as being more tolerant of people who are different from us is a positive thing for us, it is an unfortunate truth of dark psychology that we do not do that automatically. And you don't get the luxury of altering their whole kin alignment when you want to get into a person's mind for your own good.

Perhaps the entire purpose is to get them to open up more and to understand who is different from them more. This is a good objective to have. But even so, that's not a good place to start, unfortunately, because, without a great deal of time and effort, you're going to have a very hard time changing someone this drastically. Do not misinterpret us: it can be achieved, but a target like this would take a long time to be realized.

Deceiving people, that is the second essential lesson. When you construct a system, you want other people to believe in it. Even if you follow any other rule in these chapters, you can't expect them to simply believe everything you say. We need to give ourselves reasonable standards. We also need to have realistic expectations of our subject.

We have to discuss the issue where they are to a great extent. This is not just an essential dark psychology lesson. In general, it is an important lesson in communication, too: meet people where they are. Communication, if you think about it, is pretty easy. Two people exchange ideas, and if one of them wants to trick the other, they have to build a reasonably sophisticated deception that the other person will purchase. But as easy as it may sound, almost everything you might imagine could go wrong. In order for you to fail to persuade them of a lie, only one of them has to go wrong. If this occurs, it's only for one reason: while it should have, the deception did not fit into the subject's solipsistic view of the universe.

A deception that suits our own vision of the world is easy to come up with. It's another matter to think up one that makes sense to everyone else. With their deception, a successful liar must achieve two things: (1) it defines the truth as the subject is desired to perceive it, and (2) this reality fits into the present deception of the subject so that they can embrace it and see it as valid. But this just goes as far as the secrets behind convincing people that they're going to believe lies. It's an entirely different aim to convince people to follow the values and ideas that you have to have, and it's one that we'll discuss in the next chapter.

CHAPTER THIRTEEN:

HOW TO RECOGNISE WHEN MANIPULATION IS BEING USED AGAINST YOU

You can learn how to manipulate people, but it does no good if they manipulate you right back. Thankfully, as a given, you don't have to embrace their manipulative tactics because, in this chapter, we'll learn how to protect ourselves against manipulators. You have to know you are being fooled before you can defend yourself against manipulation. This is tougher than it sounds because it's not clear from the best manipulators that you are being manipulated. Right under your nose, they do their job, and you happily do what they want without even understanding it.

Finding out whether they are lying to us is the best way we can say whether we are being fooled. Now it's a huge subject in itself to find out when we are being lied to, so let's get started with it. In our chapter on reading people, telling when you are being fooled is a matter of telling when you are being lied to, and telling a liar from a truth-teller uses all the same abilities we worked on. You need a robust understanding of perceptual sharpness, the three characteristics of the cryptic language of the brain, and how implicit contact signals fit into dark psychology.

Perhaps you're not just trying to say whether anyone in life is lying about a normal situation. You may want to know if someone lies because you're trying to trick them yourself, and your fear of lying to you gets in the way. This is a positive instinct to have because if they are not painting an accurate portrait of it, you can't get into someone's mind. You're not going to be able to get into a liar's mind, so you're going to end up attempting to control the mind or manipulate a false rendition, not the actual person.

As we have said, aside from truth-tellers, the primary abilities to tell liars are the same abilities we use in any other field of dark psychology. You must pay particular attention to their body language, as always. A show of trust is the core thing that you should be searching for. Is the person trying to persuade you? You can almost know for sure that they are a fraud if you can tell them that they are making a serious attempt to get you to buy into their framing of the facts. You'd wonder if you could say if someone was "trying to persuade you of something. In reality, it's very simple: look for a difference between the way their body language is portrayed to them and that gut feeling you have about them. Maybe they're behaving like someone who is completely honest. But this is a surefire indication that they are lying if you get a poor gut feeling about them. On this one, trust your unconscious mind.

We have a word that encapsulates what is behind this difference in dark psychology. It is called Congruence, or in this case, incongruence. Congruence is how our external speech is parallel to our inner feeling; that is, how much we feel matches how we seem to feel based on the contact signals we send off.

We have gone deep into all the signs of contact already, so you already know what signs to look for here. The way we feel intuitively on the inside seems to be more complex than these signs, however. How do we know how someone on the inside

DARK PSYCHOLOGY SECRETS AND MANIPULATION

feels? We say that when there is a difference between how someone really feels and the way they portray themselves, we can tell, but how do we know for sure that our gut instinct is correct?

It's not a straightforward topic to respond to. Of course, when it comes to the unconscious mind, there is still some room for doubt. But note this: if you are told by your own unconscious mind that there is a lack of congruence between the external expression of others and the way they actually feel, you should trust that. In normal English, we may not be able to perfectly decode the language of the human mind, but our own minds speak the same language like all others, so they know when something is wrong. Listen to what you're told in your head. You may be afraid that things are bad with your unconscious mind, but the fact is, we prefer to make the opposite error. Usually, the facts are told by our unconscious minds, and our conscious minds distract our attention and prevent us from finding out the truth. Let this not happen to you.

Pay attention to the rate that the person mentioned speaks after searching for lack of congruence in the potential liar. Liars tend to speak quickly because their minds are a thousand miles per hour away. They have meticulously planned how to sell you their concept of the truth, resulting in a conversation that feels more like them giving you lots of unnecessary information about whatever it is they are selling to you. That's the other red flag that signals a liar.

The next is one you should take with a grain of salt, but we nevertheless mention it because, in the United Kingdom, it comes from a legitimate psychological study. This study looked at a group of individuals who were identified as liars or non-liars by others. One thing that the liars seemed to have in common, the scientists found: they all drank coffee.

You ought to take this with a grain of salt, as we said. Coffee is every man's drink, after all. It might simply be that everybody lies a little bit, just like everybody drinks a little bit of coffee. Just because you find out they drink coffee, there is no reason for you to jump to conclusions about someone. Yet, maybe it's something to keep in the back of your mind. For us, there are still a few more things to get into. One of them is the rate of somebody's breathing, which should not surprise you. When we tell lies, we get nervous. We need more oxygen in our bodies when we get nervous, so we have to breathe more air. Another explanation for this is that they use a lot of cognitive energy to keep track of all the stuff they need to say a good lie. This requires a lot more effort, the need for more oxygen than a regular, honest conversation with others.

Two key ways to say if anyone needs to breathe more are available. The first is that when they are speaking, their shoulders go up. This is a habit that a lot of individuals have when they need a sudden air rush. The second way to say this is when they take a big breath in the middle of a word. If you listen carefully, you will find that taking fairly loud breaths when they are talking is not all too unusual for people, particularly if they are talking for a long time. But in the middle of a sentence, it is not common for someone to take a deep breath. It's a pretty straightforward example of a liar.

Another big red flag is repetitive thoughts. Liars want to repeat themselves because they want you desperately to believe what they are doing. At this point, it is an emotional problem because they are concerned about the social consequences they will face if they are caught lying. Another reason a liar might do this is that they're trying to think about a new one and the next way out of this subject, so they're stalling. Some of these symptoms are ones that almost everyone is aware of, but we will still cover them briefly for the sake of being thorough. People may be dishonest and hardly make any eye contact at all. Remember, however, and you always have to remember the person you are referring to. If this is someone who, in the first place, barely makes eye contact, they're probably not lying. But if you're in a well-established relationship with them and they usually make regular eye contact with you, they're not now you're talking to a liar.

Fidgeting is the next well-known one. While there are some individuals who just do it as a natural, non-anxicty-related habit, fidgeting appears to be a nervous habit, so bear in mind the kind of person you talk to as usual.

But be careful that guilt over being caught in a lie often has a different dimension of it. The fight-or-flight response is often a product of anxiety. They fidget when somebody's brain chooses "fight." That may sound a little weird, but it's because we feel like we are doing something when we fidget. It's a way to get rid of the nerves that we've created.

But the other side of fight-and-flight fear is flight. They will not fidget when the liar's brain chooses flight. They're going to do the reverse: they're going to freeze. For this reason, if anyone is standing oddly still as they say things that you think are somewhat dubious, you are probably justified in believing that they are deceptive about something.

There are a couple of other signs that alert you to the fact that someone is probably a liar. After that, when you talk to someone you think may be manipulating you, we will explore other things you can look out for. If you cover your mouth a lot, there's a fair chance you're lying to them. That they don't want you to see their mouth is an unconscious warning to themselves. Of course, they don't really want you to see what you've heard coming out of their ears because you wouldn't believe it if you really heard it. This is the unconscious side of it, so they're just doing it consciously, too, because you don't see their facial expressions. They were worried that you would be able to tell them that they were lying in their faces (and you would! after reading this book).

Before we thought that someone could make too much eye contact with you to try to gain control of the social situation very hard, they attempt to be dominant at their best, but they end up with the opposite outcome. This is much worse for liars and malicious manipulators. In a sloppy effort to intimidate you from challenging them, they'll also make a lot of eye contact with you. This will work on other people, but it won't work on you as you have studied in the field of deception and mind control yourself.

When it comes to the detection of liars, there is one last trick we have for you. In fact, this could be the most significant thing you read in the novel. While you will find use in the use of dark psychology to advance your career and anywhere else, if anyone holds you down, you can't do that. And liars are the ones who are going to keep you down the most. This is the most fool-free method for testing whether or not anyone is lying. While all the others will support you, it would probably be enough if you just had this one at your disposal.

In a few quick steps, it happens. Let's claim that you're talking to a possible liar. You know then that they could be lying about something. Next, what you do is move the conversation in the direction of the thing about which you believe they are lying. Don't indict them for anything. All you have to do is demonstrate an interest in the subject matter of curiosity that you feel they are not honest about. They are likely to get nervous when you do this. In order to track their body language when they get anxious, use perceptual sharpness.

But we still haven't even reached the most critical part. After taking this subject up, step away from it absolutely. Put on a show as though you have lost interest in it absolutely as if you do not accuse them of lying at all. Let them believe that you fell for it.

This is where, most of all, you have to control their body language. You will see something drastic happen if they are lying: they will relax. Suddenly, their chest sticks up, and you'll hear a pretty noisy breath coming out. In the sound of their speech, the laid-back attitude they have afterward, they will show that they are comfortable, and so on. After you act as you fell absolutely for the lie when they lied, your unconscious mind would be able to tell a major difference in their body language. You won't see anything changing in their body language if this individual wasn't lying.

Don't be wrong with us. In detecting lies, no strategy is absolutely fool-proof. This one is as good as it comes, though, and it is pretty darn good. A very good liar might still pass this test, stop not let your guard go down completely, but if they pass this test and don't seem to be a liar, you should be able to relax a good deal.

You have done more than half the job of recognizing a dishonest manipulator, now that you know how to spot a liar. We call them malicious manipulators, and in a way, they don't just use dark psychology to profit them. They use it to support themselves and, along the way, harm you. Of course, note that there is absolutely no justification for you to hurt someone else in the process when you use dark psychology. Unfortunately, there are people that are going to do something to someone, and that's how you define these people, so you stay away from them and don't get hurt further.

Malicious deception requires a great deal of deceit, but not everything that makes it up is lying. That is why you will be alerted by the rest of the chapter of all the other signs that others are abusing you.

The first one is that the liar blames you every single time, no matter what. Not only do they not accept the blame when it is theirs—every does this sometimes. We are talking about something different there. We are talking about someone who never admits they had some fault in whatever the problem was. Once you prod them a little bit with questions, you realize something even more. Not only are they not willing to admit they are wrong about anything. They genuinely do not believe that this could happen. In their minds, they really do think they do nothing wrong, and that's why they never accept it when you say they made a mistake.

As you might expect—or as you might know, if you have dealt with someone like this—it gets immensely irritating to have someone like this in your life. Sure, all of us will refuse to accept blame sometimes. But there comes the point with a compulsive liar where you realize they aren't doing what other people do. They don't understand the mere concept of making a mistake themselves. It always has to be someone else's fault. This is how they manage to manipulate you. You may be annoyed by it at first, but you think it is an ordinary human flaw. Later on, you think perhaps they have this flaw more than the average person. But as more time passes, it's inevitable that you realize they just aren't familiar with the concept of being wrong about something.

We just called them compulsive liars, but there is another word for this person that we have already gone over in this very book. They are a solipsist. Only the rules of their personal universe apply. If the solipsist believes something doesn't apply in their private world, this is the only thing that matters to them. The solipsist—the compulsive liar—ends up bringing you into their little personal universe and convincing you of their beliefs. It takes time for you to realize you have been fooled. It even takes shelving some pride to admit it. But you are better off admitting you were wrong than staying with them any longer.

This is a good opportunity to let you in on something important when you are entering the world of dark psychology, especially as a beginner: you probably are unique indeed to entering this forbidden field of knowledge. Most people simply won't go near it because of the name alone. People who venture beyond the name still don't want to learn more about it because they are afraid of what people will think of them if they found out. You went further than all of these people did and made your way over halfway through this book. However, this fact alone does not make you immune from being manipulated by other people. At the end of the day, you need to humbly accept the fact that you are just as susceptible to being manipulated as anyone else. Of course, this isn't exactly true in a literal sense. We have already discussed how some people are more vulnerable to the techniques of dark psychology than others. If you have traits the opposite of theirs, you may be less vulnerable to it.

You can certainly still be mind-controlled and manipulated. Refusing to admit this fact will not keep it from being true. You are better off accepting you could be manipulated and defending yourself against it. After all, you don't have to resign yourself to it. You just have to be read by following our directions. As you read, you may think it would be impossible for a solipsist to drag you into the fantasy land of their unconscious mind. But trust us: stranger things have happened.

CHAPTER FIFTEEN:

BRAINWASHING, THE DAMAGE IT DOES & OTHER TECHNIQUES FOR DARK MIND CONTROL

During the Korean War, the first recorded use of the term brainwashing occurred in the 1950s and was rapidly popularized as the concept spread fear, paranoia, and all other kinds of negative emotions across all races, beliefs, and religions around the globe.

It was used to describe the process of thought reform, and persuasion used to influence the mental state of American Prisoners of War under their control by Korean and Chinese soldiers. POWs were put through a variety of brainwashing techniques during their time in foreign prison camps (most of the experimental and previously untested) until they lost their identities, converted national allegiance against their home country, and even admitted to war crimes with which they had no involvement.

Brainwashing has been a point of interest for many people since its conception and widespread acceptance as a psychological advancement, from those who want to use it, those who want to regain their control over themselves, and those who want to avoid ever coming into contact with the type of brainwashing or its many techniques and intentions.

While in the field of psychology, the term and its research may be newer, the real processes and methods used in brainwashing have been around as long as people wanted to control the way others think, feel and behave.

We'll take a closer look at brainwashing in this chapter, the fundamentals of it, and how to avoid becoming a target, especially for those who intend to do harm.

Brainwashing Basics: What Is It & How Is It Different From Other Psychological Influencing Methods?

When you look at the elements of the method and where they evolved from, brainwashing is not a new concept in psychology or even with respect to human history. Those who study it professionally sometimes call it thought reform, a title was given to the method thanks to the process involved in brainwashing someone. It is defined as the deliberate act of changing the thoughts or feelings of another individual or group of individuals against their will (and sometimes without their knowledge).

Everywhere you look, brainwashing techniques are in use, and not always for underhanded or dangerous reasons. In advertising companies or for political campaigns, some techniques are used regularly. It is hard to identify, like persuasion and manipulation, until you are completely absorbed in it.

However, brainwashing is less effective, unlike those two techniques that also have deep roots in psychology and dark psychology, unless used in large groups and with willing victims (like cults and political followers).

A quick comparison of techniques to make it easier for those new to the world of Dark Psychology to distinguish a distinction:

- When used, persuasion aims to get the target to believe that by careful thinking and increased knowledge of the situation, they have changed their own minds. People who use this technique want a change in attitude to their goals, making them feel positive about their decision to change their thoughts or behaviors. They would like to influence their future without rewriting their past.
- Manipulation is the powerful change of the thoughts and feelings of someone through aggressive pressure as a way to gain control of their actions for an egotistical and often malevolent purpose. They have no interest in their target's past or long-term future, beyond what they need to know to gain power for their own advantage over them.

Somewhere in the middle of both, brainwashing techniques lie. They are not often used with vicious intent, but due to their popularity with those who tend to use it as a means of control or power over others, the term has gained that reputation.

For the brainwasher (sometimes referred to as the agent), the ultimate aim of brainwashing is to get the subject to adjust their thoughts and emotions to their core values and past experiences in order to gain control over how they think and respond.

The main purpose of brainwashing when used for wrong or unethical means is to attack a person at their very foundation (their knowledge of who they are, their morality, and ethical opinions) and cause them to doubt themselves so that they embrace the brainwashing techniques used as truth, reassurance or validation as they try to unite their lives and the new "truths" to which they have been exposed.

In particular, more mild brainwashing versions and effective techniques have been used to sell products such as cigarettes by placing subliminal messages in films, TV shows, papers, radio, and all other types of media so that they may not be directly advertising the product.

Some of the brainwashing tricks popularized by this form of product campaign included little, but heavy, elements such as ensuring that the individual holding the cigarette in the movie or image was always smiling and laughing or using the right colors and fonts to lure people in and make them want to go straight to the store to pick up a pack.

Layers Of Lies: The Steps To Successful Brainwashing

When it comes to attempting to brainwash others, individual methods have a little successful impact. Brainwashing is a procedure that requires a carefully selected set of strategies that are calculated on the basis of the goal, the purpose, and the amount of time the agent has to accomplish their ultimate goal or the process of brainwashing. Regardless of the particulars, for those who read about, practice, and perfect their methods, the basic layers of brainwashing are consistent.

1. Rewrite The Past: When it comes to good brainwashing, this first step is the most important. Rewriting a person's past begins by challenging their values, backgrounds, and everything else they have experienced and kept close to them. If the brainwashing agent cannot challenge what they know about their target, there is no way they can implant

new information and beliefs (subliminally or forcefully). When anyone starts to doubt themselves, they become more open to new beliefs, looking in their unknown setting for answers and unexpectedly viewing the world in an ambiguous way.

2. Inspire Remorse: Guilt is a potent emotion used by brainwashing agents to further control their goals to change their perceptions, emotions, and behavioral patterns. By the end of the first level, the aim is to disregard anything they have ever thought or believed (assuming that brainwashing is successful) and the new concepts and ideas that their agents want them to accept have been introduced. While they may be reluctant to just begin to embrace new world views or immediately change their actions, once they not only reject their previous views but feel guilty about them, they are more likely to become less confrontational and more cooperative to manipulate future thinking and reality.

3. The All Is Lost Moment: For storytellers and authors who want to create a moment of vulnerability for their characters to resolve, this is a common cause. The "All Is Lost Moment" comes when a person is driven to the point of hopelessness when it comes to variables such as:

• Who they are, their character and their worldview, Where they were, and what they did to become the person they are now (the person that they are doubting and have lost all faith in)

• What they expect in the future and how they see themselves if at all, getting there.

- The high chance of suicide by the target or the chance that they will injure others after losing their respect for human life is a few of the risks of brainwashing to the point of hopelessness.

4. Reaching Out & Making An Offer: Brainwashing is a very lonely process for the target even though they are part of collective thought manipulation. Once they have been psychologically worn down to the point of hopelessness (certainly in any good brainwashing endeavor at this stage), it provides an opportunity for the agent to make an emotional bond, superficial or not, in order to gain their trust and make the final pull from their present psychological state to the way of thinking or acting of the agent. For something as easy as getting them a glass of fresh water, an extra portion of food, or something else they like, the initial connection can be made. This reflects empathy for the objective (however feigned) and makes them more open to discussion or intervention. A simple act of kindness or human moment brings the agent to a desperate target ready to change their circumstances from villain to potential ally.

5. Confession & The Compulsion to Get Involved: Seeing a way out or a way to make things better makes people want to admit that they are making the right decision by embracing anything that will make them feel better. By this stage, with little chance of breaking free before the conclusion of the plan and the consequences that follow, the target is fully under the control of the agent. They may still have hesitations, but if the process needs to be reinforced, they are far more open to persuasion and other brainwashing techniques.

6. Acceptance & Rebirth: The target completely acknowledges the brainwashing process in this final step, embraces the new truths they have been fed, and becomes the new person they have been created to be through careful preparation, teaching, manipulating, and often even physical torture (not technically a brainwashing technique, but often used in political, wartime, criminal and other darker uses of brainwashing to control prisoners, victims, and captives).

Once all these steps have been performed to their fullest (or their most efficient depending on the circumstances), then the process of brainwashing can be deemed complete and the agent can take a look at the list of events that have taken place and see how successful they have been in their efforts. Psychological studies have shown that brainwashing is one of the least powerful methods of mental and emotional control in which people can spend their time because it is so difficult, and the individual results of all the various interventions have yet to be thoroughly studied. The main question that experts have asked about brainwashing methods and have been asking since the beginning is whether a manipulation tool is as powerful as people think it is (worry or hope it is) because of the brainwashing process itself or because of the susceptibility to psychological influence of individual targets. From there, they ask questions such as what makes some people more susceptible than others and can brainwashing techniques be used with the same effect as others across genders, races, and social classes, or can certain variables and steps be lost in translation?

The Impact Of Brainwashing's Individuals And Groups

Various groups of scholars and analysts who spent years researching American soldiers who returned to the United States after being released from the war camps, but were branded as victims of brainwashing at the time of their return, have debated the impact of brainwashing itself (and how efficient it is a form of psychological control). They believed that through the physical torture and neglect they endured and not the actual brainwashing process, the ones they talked to were most likely converted. Their key justification for believing this is that, with some success, fewer than two dozen of the tens of thousands of inmates put through brainwashing trials fall under the effects. This number, however, only takes into account the soldiers who wanted to return to the United States, not those who were so turned against their home country that they decided to stay in their captors' lands long after the war had ended and all were freed.

In the continued interest of brainwashing and its consequences, cults around the world have played a significant role. It is easy to tell from the outside that cults are strange and difficult to understand why someone would want to get involved in one, but some of the most practiced and well-tested agents and manipulators in human society are brainwashing, coercion, and other influential psychological influence methods by the leaders or recruiters of these organizations. The key way they achieve this is by approaching individuals who are most open to manipulation, making them unique and part of a group, and then convincing them that what they do or stand for is truly right and good through fake friendship or understanding.

In the long run, effective brainwashing can have a variety of impacts on people and groups of individuals. Some of the most common side effects that can be relieved or reversed by an un-brainwashing phase (more commonly referred to as deprogramming) include:

- Broken sense of confidence—This can also lead to a series of painful and risky choices, such as alcohol dependency or the use of stronger drugs.
- Inability to trust individuals—People who have survived the brainwashing process (successful or otherwise) tend to disappear into themselves, unaware of how to trust people they are surrounded by after their ordeal, from any random experience to those they love with all their heart.
- They see everything as a test—A lot of life loses its excitement after a brainwashing process. The victim rarely shows any interest in events or hobbies they once loved, losing their drive and hope for the future.

They pause and make sure to tear apart and evaluate every aspect every time they are given an opportunity or asked to engage in a challenge before even worrying about whether or not it is something they want to take part in.

How To Defend Yourself From Being The Victim Of Malicious Techniques Of Brainwashing

Who is most vulnerable to strategies for brainwashing? Who is most likely to become a target of those trying to boost their standing or just tear down others by persuading people (sometimes a full flip) to change their view of the world?

One of the most common reasons people get drawn into cults or into a coercive agent's influence is that they have no idea what brainwashing really looks like or what kinds of warning signs to look for. The first way to defend yourself from these types of psychological predators from falling prey is to know the attributes they are searching for in potential targets, such as:

- Loners who have never found their place but have not given up on discovering where or who they fit in with. This is one of the reasons why these runaway teens are frequently targeted by cult brainwashing and related gangs. In certain situations, they have not yet generated the moral maturity or life experience to know they are being taken advantage of.
- They have nobody to stand up for them. This may be because, by default, they are anti-social, but it is more likely because they are too stubborn to take others' advice and appear to become aggressive when they are told what to do or should be more careful
- They look for responses or for a reason. This is when friends, family members, mentors, or someone they know or have come to admire and trust are drawn into future goals. In situations like this, the agent uses their knowledge of the goal and their perception of how they see the world to gain control over them.
- The first step is to provide their objective with a sense of obligation to get them on board with the brainwashing process, which is then accompanied by motivating feelings of remorse and disappointment in the goal when they hesitate or fail in their assigned mission.

Nobody feels that they're open to brainwashing. The idea itself, in fact, conjures visions of malnourished inmates forced to watch propaganda videos before they embrace them as truth and captured spies being injected with transparent liquids that alter their mental state in order to change their reality through chemical means. Brainwashing, however, is not always as drastic but can also be as damaging and hazardous. The next step is to look for warning signs that brainwashing is happening around you once a person has decided whether or not they have the potential to become a victim. Some of the most popular and frequently produced include:

- Unknown, confounding, and sometimes growing sense of fear connected with the world outside their home or wherever they currently reside
- The constant sense of inadequacy even though they realize that they have done their absolute best
- Feelings of mistrust and anxiety struggle over not impossible, but often unlikely events such as natural disasters striking out of nowhere, the fear of terrorist attacks at each location they visit from public toilets in their local grocery store to the sidewalk corner across from their living quarters
- Abandonment of contact devices (no mobile phone or social media permitted) and disconnection from individuals with whom they are normally social

CONCLUSION

Now that you can recognize what dark psychology is all about and who the manipulators may be in your life (or whether you've been guilty of using these techniques as well), identify signs of being manipulated, and learn how to handle them, you can better evaluate the relationships around you to make the healthy choices you need in your own life. Through a more realistic view of life, you may share your thoughts, opinions, and wishes without feeling guilty, realizing that they are truly your own.

You can detect and understand the signals of persuasion and manipulation by evaluating and examining the contact signs in your relationships. When that is evident, you will exercise your right to be treated with dignity. In a contact exchange, you regain the power and right to be equal individuals to yourself. In a relationship with an equal balance of control, you CAN say 'no' without feeling guilty and CAN set your goals to build a better life or world for yourself and others you care for.

The ability to interpret people's body language and see beyond misleading phrases stops you from being extorted or abused unknowingly. You are more open to opportunities around you and less likely to be affected by others' purpose and motivated by it. But being able to identify those tactics means that you too can manipulate these tricks. Be sure to consult with your moral compass and be constantly mindful of treating each person as an equal citizen, worthy of the right to be treated and free to choose.

The principle of Dark Psychology assumes possibly you're ignorant of previous devious actions or just do not care. Here's an opportunity to change the trajectory of yours and start anew. Whatever predatory actions you've engaged in, criminal and sociopathic, there's usually a decision to cease, desist, and part from the abyss of getting sociopathic.

The capability of the head might be said to be very vast, and this might be said that the individuals that see how the mind of theirs functions might have a tendency to get much more out of life. Additionally, learning how you can take control of the mind of yours might enable you to be in charge of the points that occur in daily life. Thus, rather than allowing life to come about for you, you can decide what goes on in that life of yours. The survivalist mentality is the norm of ours, and what society tries to do is actually manage the wild beast in each and every man by teaching them out of an early age to obey the laws, morals, and rules of the controlling team, typically the rich, who dominate our institutions and governments.

Thus, must we condemn the ones that think society isn't providing them a good offer—which they need to take whatever they have to endure an often hostile atmosphere in which privilege relies on the school of yours, wealth, or loved ones? The dark Psychology Secret itself really needs to come out of the closet and acknowledge that the typical human action is actually opposing rules and society.

The individuals resent society, but since they're powerless against people who control law-making and morality, they think of specific helplessness in looking to live amongst the sheep. Could it be any wonder then sometimes a private person takes it and create their own hands to change society or maybe the environment of theirs to live a freer self-controlled existence from the rigors of communities which, as we've seen, all eventually breakdown and reinvent themselves as the powerful and rich newly take control again? All empires can't see their demise! Exactly how will Dark Psychology Secret then contend with this particular question of human behavior like a simple survivalist mechanism, in which humans are obviously brutal, harsh, and dominating of others that are weaker than themselves?

Psychiatry in mental hospitals is frequently viewed as the element of societal control—in case you don't go along with society as well as the rules of it is you then should be insane—for that reason, you need to be dedicated as well as managed for the security as well as the advantage of all. On the additional hand, Dark Psychology Secret is actually viewed as the liberating part of psychological health—the place we help those out of synch with the society of finding the place of theirs and fit back into what's regarded behavior that is ordinary for that team. Anywhere will the solution be for individuals who rebel against the society they live in and would like another method of presence without the interference of the effective as well as the independence to live a life they select as suiting themselves. Or perhaps do we wait—for the films to come true the disaster that awaits a return, as well as all humans to a dog, called survivalism—the genuine cultural majority! Around this junction, it's some time to determine from these observations which societal norms, laws, and morals are, in fact, "not normal" for man, and this society typically forces group conduct depending on what the highly effective want with the powerless.

Finally, Thank You For Reading This Fantastic Book!

If you found this book useful in any way, we always appreciate a review on Amazon!

Made in the USA
Las Vegas, NV
26 September 2023

78163216R00098